JUDY
JOO'S
# KOREAN
# SOUL
# FOOD

**To my amazing Dad, Dr. Eui Don Joo,**
**for his 80th birthday.**

Thank you for being the best Daddy ever, and for teaching
me the importance of hard work, kindness, love,
and giving me an intrepid spirit.

# JUDY JOO'S

# KOREAN SOUL FOOD

with Mi Kyung Jeong

Photography by
Yuki Sugiura

WHITE LION PUBLISHING

# CONTENTS

# CONTENTS

# JUDY JOO'S

# KOREAN SOUL FOOD

with Mi Kyung Jeong

Photography by
Yuki Sugiura

WHITE LION
PUBLISHING

# Introduction

I am a French-trained, Korean American Londoner; my recipes deeply reflect my multicultural upbringing and life. I consider myself a true global citizen, embracing various cultures and traditions.

I am the daughter of Korean immigrant parents, and am proudly dedicating this book to my father for his 80th birthday.

My father was born in Chongju, a small coastal village between Sinuiju and Pyongyang, in what is now North Korea. In 1945, the communists invaded, and seized his father's land, forcing them to pack up what they could carry, and flee south with his eight siblings. Even at just six years old, my dad had to haul his share – a small backpack full of fine silk to be used to barter their way onto trains heading south and to buy safe passage through Russian-occupied territory. They took a train to Haeju, then crossed the southern border. They escaped under the cover of darkness, wading through the sea's low tide to Kaesong, which was then part of South Korea. In 1950, the Korean War broke out and my dad's family fled further and sought refuge on Jeju island. My father was too young to be drafted, but four of his older brothers were enlisted. My dad grew up in a refugee camp on this small volcanic island, which is now ironically a popular holiday destination. He remembers looking up at tall, smartly-clad US soldiers and begging them for 'bon bons'.

From this challenging situation, he somehow managed through hard work to make it to the 'Harvard' of Korea and attended Seoul National University Medical School. From there he immigrated to the USA in 1967 for his internship and residency in Psychiatry in New York City.

He was introduced to my mom, whose older brother was my dad's classmate. She had travelled to the US alone (unheard of in those days) to get her master's degree in Chemistry at Ohio University. They got married in 1970, and are still together. My sister, Sonya, came along a few years later, and then they moved to New Jersey, where I was born.

My mom had to make everything from scratch to get that taste of home they so desperately craved. Our porch was crowded with pots teeming full of fermenting delicacies. Our garage boasted hangers of drying seaweed and our picnic table often showcased chillies basking in the sun. A small garden at the end of our yard produced a bounty of perilla leaves, chillies and Korean squash. And, every now and then, large packages from Korea would arrive, stuffed full of coveted culinary treasures, such as dried seaweed, anchovies and persimmons.

I grew up eating glorious home cooking made with the love of my mother's hands and heart. I often watched my mom make huge vats of kimchi, and my sister and I were regularly enslaved to make hundreds of dumplings at a time. I remember her scooping up a small bite of whatever she was making and feeding us directly from her fingers. Food was, and still is, a language of love for her, and it has become one of mine too.

I learned so much from my mom, and through my travels, and my time in the USA, Korea and the UK, I have embraced various cooking techniques and ingredients, many of which you'll see reflected in this book. I hope my recipes feed your soul, satiate your tummy, and make you and your loved ones smile.

# Korean Storecupboard

**1  Dashima**  (dried kelp)
These dried flat sheets of seaweed are used with dried anchovies and mushrooms to make a traditional Korean stock. Also known as kombu, this kelp is full of umami flavour and adds great depth and complexity.

**2  Pyogo Beoseot**  (dried shiitake mushrooms)
I always add these richly flavoured mushrooms to my Korean stock to boost flavour even more, especially when making a vegetarian version.

**3  Gochujang**  (Korean chilli paste)
This fermented chilli paste is one of the cornerstones of Korean cooking, and there really is no substitute. Bright, fiery red in colour, but not overly spicy, this thick unctuous paste is used in various ways. It is made with gochugaru (Korean chilli paste), dried fermented soy bean powder, salt, sweet glutinous rice powder and usually a sweetener (honey or sugar). Recipes can vary depending on region, but it is always fermented and the resultant flavour is richly deep and distinctive.

**4  Mirin or Mirim**  (Korean cooking wine)
Sweet and light with a low alcohol content, mirin adds a hint of nectarous flavour to many dishes.

**5  Gyeoja**  (Korean mustard)
Similar to English mustard, gyeoja is bright yellow and hot and spicy. Available in both in powder and paste form, it is used in dressings and as a side condiment.

**6  Daechu**  (dried jujube dates)
Dried jujubes boast an eye-catching shiny, dark-red skin, and a balanced, moderately sweet taste. Also called Chinese dates, these dried fruits are used in both savoury and sweet cooking. You can now buy them dehydrated and sliced, which makes for great snacking and garnish.

**7  Yujacha**  (citron tea syrup)
This citron fruit and honey syrup resembles marmalade, but is much more fragrant and luxurious in flavour. Yuja fruit, or yuzu in Japanese, tastes like the offspring of a bergamot lemon and a satsuma mandarin. It is traditionally used to make tea, but I use it for a number of different dishes.

**8  Dwengjang**  (Korean soy bean paste)
Deeply flavoured and dark brown, this rich, fermented, pungent paste is stronger and coarser than its Japanese counterpart, miso. Red miso can be used as a substitute, but dwengjang does have its own unique taste that makes it worth stocking.

**9  Myulchi** (dried anchovies)
These little fish come in a myriad of different sizes and are used in various ways. This larger variety is used primarily for infusing flavour into broths. My mom always removed the heads and the guts to prevent bitter undertones.

**10  Kkae** (black and white sesame seeds)
Sesame seeds are used liberally in Korean cooking. White ones are more common and can be bought pre-roasted in large shaker jars. I also like to buy kkaesogeum (sesame seed salt), which is a mix of half crushed roasted seeds with salt, perfect for seasoning everything from banchan side dishes to barbecue.

**11  Saewoojeot** (salted shrimp)
These tiny, heavily salted shrimp are an essential ingredient for making kimchi, but are also used to make banchan (side dishes) and in soups and stews.

**12  Ganjang** (soy sauce)
Soy sauce is a by-product of making dwengjang, and can be fermented for years, developing in taste and complexity much like an aged balsamic vinegar. There are many types, with the darker varieties being used for heartier fare and soups and stews, and the lighter versions for more delicate dishes. Use soy sauce to add seasoning and flavour, but it does not always replace the need for salt entirely.

**13  Chamgireum** (sesame oil)
Dark brown in colour and nutty in flavour, this fragrant oil is made from roasted and ground sesame seeds. It has a very unique earthy taste that makes it great to use in dressings and marinades. I like to add just a drizzle to finish many of my dishes, to give them an enticing toasty aroma.

**14  Gochugaru** (Korean chilli flakes)
Brightly coloured, these flakes made from Korean chillies come in several varieties in both grind size and spiciness level. They are an essential ingredient of many dishes, namely kimchi. Go for the coarsely ground, medium spicy kind and sprinkle freely on anything; it's your go-to chilli flake for a bit of kick and vibrant colour.

# Sauces

*I serve most of the sauces for my recipes on the side, so that the diner can decide how much they want. These sauces are quite versatile, so don't be afraid to try them for different dishes than those suggested in this book.*

### 1 Chilli-Soy Dipping Sauce
*Yangnyum Ganjang*

6 tbsp soy sauce
2½ tbsp sagwa-shikcho (Korean apple vinegar)
  or rice wine vinegar
1 tbsp thinly sliced Korean red chilli,
  sliced at an angle
4 tsp roasted sesame oil
2 tsp roasted sesame seeds
2 spring onions,
  very thinly sliced at an angle

### 2 Ssamjang Sauce

1 spring onion, finely chopped
2 garlic cloves, grated or finely chopped
180g (6¼oz) dwengjang (Korean soy bean paste)
4 tbsp roasted white sesame seeds
100g (3½oz) gochujang (Korean chilli paste)
75ml (2½fl oz) mirin
1½ tbsp roasted sesame oil

### 3 Pancake Dipping Sauce
### (Soy Vinaigrette Dipping Sauce)
*Choganjang*

75ml (2½fl oz) soy sauce
1½ tbsp rice wine vinegar
1 tbsp roasted sesame oil
1 tbsp roasted sesame seeds, crushed
2 tsp gochugaru (Korean chilli flakes)
1½ spring onions, finely chopped

### 4 Gochujang Mayonnaise

2 tsp gochujang (Korean chilli paste)
2 tsp Sriracha
6 tbsp Kewpie mayonnaise
½ tsp yuja juice

### Gochujang Mustard

4 tbsp wholegrain Dijon mustard
1 tsp gochujang (Korean chilli paste)

To make the above five sauces, in a small bowl mix all of the ingredients for your chosen sauce together. Cover and store in the fridge if not using immediately.

### 5 Gochujang Sauce

5 tbsp gochujang (Korean chilli paste)
4 tsp brown sugar
2 tbsp roasted sesame oil
2 tsp mirin
2 tsp water

In the small saucepan, whisk all of the ingredients together and bring to a simmer. Simmer for 3–4 minutes until thickened.

15

# SALADS & BANCHAN

Korean food is all about the sides, and these little plates are what makes Korean dining so unique. The table is laid corner to corner with small dishes, showcasing everything from vegetables, to marinated meats, to delicately fried pancakes, and more. Banchan is essential to every Korean meal in achieving a balance of flavours, textures and colours.

# Kale and Spinach Salad

## with miso black pepper dressing

*I love the heartiness of kale, but it can be hard to chew. Shredding it is a great way to lighten this rather thick leaf. The peppery dressing also lifts the earthiness of kale with some heat, and the kiss of Parmesan adds a little bit of rich, flavourful saltiness.*

**Serves 4**

170g (6oz) purple and green kale,
  stems removed and shredded
juice of ½ lemon
60g (2½oz) baby spinach
2 tbsp flaked almonds, toasted
1 tbsp pumpkin seeds, toasted
1 tbsp pine nuts, toasted
handful of Lotus Crisps
1 tbsp freshly grated Parmesan

MISO BLACK PEPPER DRESSING
1½ tbsp shallots, finely chopped
2½ tbsp soy sauce
2 tsp white miso
4 tsp rice wine vinegar
½ tsp white sugar
½ tsp English mustard
1 tbsp roasted sesame oil
1 tbsp vegetable oil (or any neutral oil)
23 twists of the black pepper mill

LOTUS CRISPS
175g (6oz) lotus roots, peeled and sliced
  into 3mm (⅛in) thick pieces
vegetable oil for deep frying
sea salt

To make the salad, place the shredded kale in a large bowl and toss with the lemon juice. Massage the kale well with your hands for about 1 minute and set aside to soften for about 3–4 minutes to break down the chewy fibres.

In a small bowl, whisk together all of the dressing ingredients and set aside.

To make the lotus crisps, heat 5cm (2in) of oil in a wide heavy-based saucepan, at least 13cm deep, over a medium–high heat until it reaches 180°C (350°F). Working in the batches, slip the lotus roots slices one by one into the oil. Fry for 2 minutes, stirring occasionally, until oil has stopped bubbling and the chips are golden brown. Transfer to wire rack or kitchen paper lined tray to drain and immediately season with salt.

Add the baby spinach and dressing to the kale. Toss together to coat, then top with the toasted almond slices, pumpkin seeds, pine nuts, lotus crisps and the freshly grated Parmesan. Finish with a bit of black pepper.

# Tomato and Avocado Salad

## with Korean mustard vinaigrette

*Avocados have been so en vogue, and this light, vibrant salad kicks it up a notch with a slightly spicy, lively mustard vinaigrette. Definitely try to find heirloom tomatoes, as the bright colours elevate this salad into something extraordinary. This dressing works well for any salad and even as a dip for prawns or crudités.*

**Serves 2**

15 cherry tomatoes or 4–5 heritage
   tomatoes (mixed colours, if available)
1 avocado, cut in half, peeled and pitted
coriander cress and amaranth cress,
   to garnish

KOREAN MUSTARD VINAIGRETTE
2½ tbsp rice wine vinegar
1 tbsp extra virgin olive oil
½ tbsp roasted sesame oil
2 tsp gyeoja (Korean mustard)
   or English mustard
1 tsp white sugar
sea salt

To make the vinaigrette, in a small bowl, whisk all the ingredients together until the sugar has dissolved and the vinaigrette is emulsified. Cover and store in the fridge if not to be used immediately.

Slice the cherry tomatoes in half. Cut the avocado into similar sized pieces. Place the avocado and tomato into a large bowl and toss around with a bit of sea salt. Then, drizzle over the vinaigrette as desired. Garnish with coriander cress and amaranth cress to serve.

# Vegetarian Dashi Stock

*This veggie stock is light, but has a deep flavour. Just add soy sauce, if you want to use it for a soup base.*

½ onion, roughly chopped
4 dried shiitake mushrooms
50g (2oz) mu (Korean white radish),
   sliced
1 spring onion, roughly chopped
13cm (5in) piece of dashima
   (dried kelp)

In a large saucepan with a lid, combine the onion, dried mushrooms, mu, spring onion, dashima and 750 ml (26fl oz) water and bring to the boil over a high heat. Reduce the heat to a simmer, cover with the lid and cook for about 45 minutes. Using a sieve, strain the stock, discarding the solids, and set aside.

# Korean-style Cucumber Salad

## Oi Muchim

*My mom used to make this salad often as it is so easy, but super tasty. The combination of spice with the tang of rice wine vinegar makes for a completely addictive side dish. Try using this dressing for other vegetables and fruits, including fresh spinach leaves, radishes and even apples.*

1 tsp kosher salt
1 tbsp gochugaru (Korean chilli flakes)
1 spring onion, thinly sliced at an angle
1 tsp garlic, grated or finely chopped
3 tbsp rice wine vinegar
2 tbsp white sugar
1 tsp roasted sesame seeds
1 tsp roasted sesame oil
2 Kirby ridged pickling cucumbers, halved lengthways, deseeded and sliced into 5mm (¼in) thick pieces

**Serves 4 (as a side dish)**

In a small bowl, whisk together the salt, gochugaru, spring onion, garlic, rice wine vinegar, sugar, sesame seeds and sesame oil until fully incorporated and the sugar is dissolved.

Toss in the cucumber slices and mix to coat. For best results, allow the cucumbers to marinate for at least 30 minutes in the fridge before serving.

# Braised Lotus Roots

## Yeongeun Jorim

*Lotus roots, with their watering-can lacework pattern, always make an elegant addition to the table. This traditional sweet, almost candied side dish is so addictive with a fresh crunch, you'll want to keep some in the fridge at all times.*

1 tbsp white wine vinegar or rice wine vinegar
400g (14oz) lotus root, peeled and sliced into 3mm (⅛in) thick pieces
300ml (10fl oz) Vegetarian Dashi Stock (page 22)
100ml (3½fl oz) soy sauce
140ml (4¾fl oz) mirin
60g (2½oz) brown sugar
2 tbsp honey
100ml (3½fl oz) mulyeot (Korean malt syrup)
2 tsp roasted sesame oil

**Serves 6 (as a side dish)**

In a large saucepan, heat 1.25 litres (2¼ pints) water with the vinegar until it boils. Add the lotus root and blanch for 1 minute, uncovered. Drain in a colander placed in a sink, rinse under cold running water and strain.

In a medium saucepan, pour in the dashi stock, soy sauce, mirin and sugar, and bring to the boil. Add the lotus roots and cook for another 10 minutes. Reduce the heat and simmer for 30 minutes until softened and the liquid is reduced by half. Occasionally turn the lotus roots over so that they cook evenly. Add the honey and mulyeot and stir. Cook for another 10 minutes.

Remove from the heat, stir in the sesame oil and serve.

# Seasoned Spinach

## Siguemchi Namul

*Mature spinach with its sweet purple roots has a heartier, meatier texture than its baby variety. My grandmother used to feed me small bites of this nutritious side dish with her fingers straight into my mouth while she was making it. She always mixed the spinach leaves with her hands to ensure the dressing was evenly coated.*

**Serves 4 (as a side dish)**

450g (1lb) mature spinach with
  stem and roots
sea salt

DRESSING
2 tbsp roasted sesame oil
1 tbsp soy sauce
1 tsp spring onion, finely chopped
1 tsp roasted sesame seeds, crushed
1 tsp sagwa-shikcho (Korean apple
  vinegar)
1 tsp brown sugar
1 garlic clove, grated or finely chopped
black pepper, freshly ground

Fill a large saucepan with water, salt well and bring to the boil. In a large bowl, prepare an ice bath.

Rinse the spinach with cold water to remove any dirt, especially around the roots. Remove any hairs from the roots. Cut the spinach into 7cm (2¾in) long pieces, keeping the purple roots intact. Split the roots in half horizontally and keep separately.

In a medium bowl, combine the dressing ingredients and stir until the sugar has dissolved. Set aside.

Blanch the spinach in two separate batches. In the boiling salt water, blanch the spinach stems with leaves until just wilted, about 1 minute, remove the spinach from the water and plunge in the ice bath. Repeat with the spinach stems with roots, but cook for 1–2 minutes before plunging into the ice bath. Remove from the ice bath, drain well and gently squeeze out any excess water.

Gently loosen the clumps of spinach with your fingers and transfer to a bowl. Toss well with the dressing. Cover and chill for about an hour to allow the flavours to mellow before serving.

# Aubergine Banchan

## Gaji Namul

*I love the silkiness of aubergines, and I have many memories of eating this colourful side dish. I remember watching my mom sauté the aubergine with chopsticks very carefully, so as not to bruise or discolour them. Asian aubergines work best for this recipe as their skins are thinner and they are much sweeter in taste.*

**Serves 6 (as a side dish)**

3 Asian aubergines, cut into finger-sized
  batons about 5cm (2in) long
½ tbsp salt
vegetable oil, for cooking
sea salt

SAUCE
2 garlic chives, chopped into
  2.5cm (1in) lengths
1 spring onion, thinly sliced at an angle
1 tsp garlic, grated or finely chopped
1 tsp gochugaru (Korean chilli flakes)
2 tsp roasted sesame seeds, crushed
½ tbsp white sugar
2 tbsp soy sauce
2 tbsp roasted sesame oil

In a large bowl, gently toss the aubergine with the salt. Place in a single layer in a colander over a plate or in a sink and allow the excess water to drain off for about 25–30 minutes.

Meanwhile, to make the sauce, whisk together all the ingredients in a small bowl. Set aside.

Shake the aubergines over the sink to remove any last drops of water.

Drizzle oil into a large non-stick frying pan, enough to coat the bottom of the pan, and place over a medium heat. Toss in the aubergine and sauté for about 2–3 minutes until just wilted. Lower the heat and, trying not to brown the aubergine, sauté for about 3 minutes until it is soft. Remove from the heat and place into a large bowl, discarding any excess oil.

Pour the sauce over the aubergine and toss to coat well. Season with salt to taste.

# Stir-Fried Korean Courgette

## Hobak Namul

*Korean courgettes are sweeter, yellower in colour and have a crunchier texture compared to their Western counterpart. You'll love their firm flesh and gorgeous green yellow hue. This classic side dish is always the most popular banchan on the table.*

**Serves 4 (as a side dish)**

2 hobak (Korean courgette) or regular
  courgettes
2 tbsp perilla oil
2 tsp garlic, grated or finely chopped
1 tbsp saewoojeot (salted shrimp)
1 tsp mirin
2 tbsp Dashi Stock
1 tbsp roasted sesame seeds, crushed
1½ spring onions, thinly sliced at an angle
1 red chilli, deseeded and thinly sliced
  at an angle
sea salt and freshly ground black pepper

Slice the hobak lengthways into 1.5cm (½in) thick slices, and then lay them down to slice again crossways and make 2.5mm (⅛in) thick pieces.

To a medium non-stick frying pan, add the perilla oil, then the chopped garlic. Cook over a low heat until just softened. Add the courgette and cook, stirring often with a wooden spoon, until just wilted. Add the saewoojeot, mirin and dashi stock. Cook for about 3–4 minutes until the courgette is softened, but remains firm. Add the sesame seeds, spring onions and chilli and toss well. Remove from the heat and season with black pepper and salt to taste.

# Dashi Stock

*Like chicken broth in Western cooking, this basic stock is used ubiquitously throughout Korean cooking. Use it in place of water as a base to add extra flavour to soups and stews.*

½ onion, roughly chopped
4 dried shiitake mushrooms
1 spring onion, roughly chopped
13cm (5in) piece of dashima
  (dried kelp)
4 myulchi (large dried anchovies),
  heads and guts removed

In a large saucepan with a lid, combine the onion, dried mushrooms, spring onion, dashima and myulchi with 750 ml (26fl oz) water and bring to the boil over a high heat. Reduce the heat to a simmer, cover with the lid and cook for about 45 minutes. Using a sieve, strain the stock, discarding the solids, and set aside.

# Egg Soufflé with Mushrooms and Truffle

## Gyeran Jjim

*Gyeran jjim is a bit of a homier version of its Japanese counterpart* chawanmushi. *My mom used to just cook hers right over the burner and let it bubble and boil, creating a bit of a crust on the bottom and a denser texture. I like to steam mine, to keep it a little lighter and silkier.*

**Serves 4**

4 shiitake mushrooms, stems removed and sliced into 5mm (¼in) pieces
vegetable oil, for frying
8 large eggs
200ml (7fl oz) Dashi Stock (page 29)
1 tsp mirin
1 tbsp soy sauce
½ bunch enoki mushrooms, trimmed of roots using just the top parts, cut into 2cm (¾in) lengths
sea salt

TO SERVE
truffle oil
chopped chives
shaved truffle

In a small non-stick frying pan drizzled with oil, sauté the shiitake mushrooms with a pinch of salt until wilted, browned and slightly dry. Move to a plate to drain. Divide the mushrooms evenly between four 280ml (10fl oz) heatproof bowls or ramekins.

In a large bowl, whisk the eggs, stock, mirin and soy sauce together. Pour the mixture through a fine sieve and divide into the four ramekins. Cover the ramekins with clingfilm and arrange them in a large wide steamer pot with a lid. Add enough boiling water so that it reaches halfway up the pot. Bring the water to a gentle low simmer, cover the pot and steam for 10 minutes until the custards are slightly wobbly in the centre.

Remove the clingfilm and divide the enoki mushrooms between the ramekins, placing them on top of the custards. Cover with the clingfilm again and steam for a further 3 minutes until the custards are set. They will puff up, but will collapse once removed from the heat. Carefully remove the ramekins from the pot.

Top the custards with a drizzle of truffle oil, a sprinkle of chives and shaved truffle, if you wish. Serve warm.

# Spam French Fries

## with Cheesy Kimchi Dipping Sauce

*Spam has a long, beloved history in Korea due to the war. Brought over as an army ration, this tinned meat product has remained a popular stalwart in Korean cuisine. My mom used to feed me fried Spam and eggs for breakfast, and rice porridge (jook) studded with cubes of Spam as an after-school snack.*

**Makes 24 fries**

350g (12oz) can of Spam
80g (3oz) plain flour
2 eggs, lightly beaten
160g (5¾oz) panko breadcrumbs
vegetable oil, for frying

CHEESY KIMCHI DIPPING SAUCE
1 tbsp cornflour
340ml (12fl oz) evaporated milk
125g (4oz) extra mature Cheddar
  cheese, grated
100g (3½oz) Parmesan, grated
3–4 tbsp cabbage kimchi and juice,
  chopped into 5mm (¼in) pieces

First, make the cheesy kimchi dipping sauce. In a small saucepan placed over a low heat, whisk together the cornflour and the evaporated milk until smooth. Turn up the heat to low–medium and cook, while continuously whisking, to thicken. Once thickened and bubbling, reduce the heat to low and stir in the cheeses and kimchi. Let the cheese melt slowly while stirring continuously to prevent burning. Cook until smooth and velvety. Add more milk if necessary to achieve the desired consistency. Keep in a warm place.

Cut the block of Spam lengthways into six slices, and cut each slice into four even matchsticks.

To batter the Spam sticks, set up three dipping stations: spread out the flour on a dinner plate; in a small, wide bowl, whisk the eggs; and on another dinner plate, pour out the panko breadcrumbs.

Coat each Spam stick with the flour and shake off the excess. Then dip into the egg wash. Lastly, coat the Spam stick with the panko breadcrumbs.

Heat about 10cm (4in) of oil in a wide heavy-based saucepan to 180°C (350°F) using a frying thermometer. Working in small batches, fry the Spam sticks until golden brown. Place on a rack to drain the oil. Serve immediately with the cheesy kimchi dipping sauce on the side.

# PICK LES &KIM CHI

Preserved and fermented foods have
a long history in Korea. Kimchi, a style
of fermented vegetables or fruits,
is the cornerstone of Korean cuisine,
and is traditionally eaten every
day with each meal.

# Whole Radish Kimchi

## Chonggak Kimchi

*My favourite types of kimchi are made with radishes, as they provide a much crunchier and satisfying bite. This version uses whole small radishes along with their sweet tops. This kimchi is traditionally served whole, and then cut up using scissors at the table.*

**Makes a 2.5 litre (4¼ pint) jar**

2kg (4lb 8oz) chonggakmu (ponytail radishes) or baby daikon radishes, stems intact and radishes peeled
75g (3oz) coarse sea salt
185g (6½oz) gochugaru (Korean chilli flakes)
85g (3oz) garlic, peeled and roots removed
65g (2½oz) ginger, peeled and roughly chopped
2 spring onions, trimmed and roughly chopped
2 tbsp Korean anchovy sauce
1 tsp sea salt
35g (1¼oz) brown sugar
85ml (3fl oz) Dashi Stock (page 29) or water
65g (2½oz) wild chives, cut into 3cm (1¼in) lengths

In a large bowl, toss together the radishes and salt, and add just enough water to cover. Leave to stand at room temperature overnight.

Drain off and discard the salted water. Rinse the radishes well with cold water 4–5 times to remove the salt, then gently squeeze out any excess moisture. Set aside the radishes in a colander and leave to drain for at least 30 minutes.

In a food processor, place the gochugaru, garlic, ginger, spring onions, anchovy sauce, salt, sugar and stock and process until a paste forms, then stir in the chives.

Mix the spice mixture with the radishes, covering them evenly and coating the leaves on both sides. Transfer to a clean 2.5 litre (4¼ pint) jar or other non-reactive container, packing them in firmly. Cover tightly and allow to ferment at room temperature for 24 hours (the optimum temperature for fermentation is 65°C/18°F) then transfer to a fridge. The kimchi is ready to eat immediately but for best flavour, ferment for about 2–3 weeks before eating.

# White Kimchi

## Baek Kimchi

*Contrary to popular belief, not all kimchi is spicy. This white version is refreshing and crisp and often eaten in the summertime. The pickling liquid is so tasty, and rather revitalizing on a hot day; you'll often see people 'drinking' it by the spoonful.*

**Makes about 5 litres (8.8 pints)**

230g (8oz) sea salt

1 very large Korean cabbage or several heads Chinese cabbage (2.2–2.7kg/5–6lb total weight), bottom(s) trimmed, wilted or tough outer leaves discarded, and rinsed well

20g (¾oz) sweet rice flour

KIMCHI PASTE

1 large Asian pear, grated, juice and pulp reserved

1 small onion, grated, juice and pulp reserved

4 tsp garlic, grated or finely chopped

2 tsp ginger, grated or finely chopped

2½ tbsp sea salt

½ leek, cut into 5cm (2in) lengths and julienned

450g (1lb) mu (Korean white radish) or mooli, peeled and julienned

1 carrot, julienned

1 red chilli, deseeded and julienned lengthways

1 green chilli, deseeded and julienned lengthways

30g (1oz) daechu (dried jujube dates), deseeded and julienned

20g (¾oz) pine nuts

In a large bowl, stir together 2 litres (3½ pints) warm water and 115g (4oz) of the salt until it has dissolved; leave it to cool. Meanwhile, partially cut the cabbage in half lengthways, starting from the root end and cutting about halfway to the top. Pull the cabbage apart to split in half completely. Repeat, keeping the leaves intact and whole.

Loosen the leaves of each wedge. Sprinkle the remaining 115g (4oz) salt over and between all the leaves, salting the core area heavily. Put the cabbage in a large bowl (use two if they don't fit) cut-side up. Pour the salted water over the cabbage, then add cold water to cover the cabbage; don't overfill the bowl. Weigh it down with a plate. Leave at room temperature for 6–8 hours, flipping the wedges halfway through.

Rinse the wedges well under cold running water and gently squeeze out any excess moisture. Put the cabbage cut-side down, in a colander and leave to drain for at least 30 minutes.

Meanwhile, make a starch paste. In a small saucepan, stir together 200ml (7fl oz) water and the sweet rice flour. Cook over a medium heat, stirring frequently, for about 4–5 minutes until it thickens and starts to bubble. Transfer the mixture to a bowl and leave to cool.

In a separate bowl, stir together 80g (3oz) of the starch paste with the kimchi paste ingredients. Rub the paste over the wedges and between each leaf. Pull the outer leaf of each wedge tightly over the rest of it, to form a tidy parcel. Pack into a container with a tight-fitting lid and press down well to avoid air pockets. Add 250ml (8fl oz) water to the bowl used for the paste, then pour into the kimchi container. Press a piece of clingfilm on to the surface of the kimchi, then cover. The kimchi can be eaten at this stage, or leave it to sit at room temperature for about 2–3 days until it starts to sour and 'bubble'.

Store the kimchi in the fridge, where it will continue to ferment at a slower pace. Cut the kimchi before serving.

# Broccoli, Romanesco and Cauliflower Water Kimchi

## Mul Kimchi

*Water kimchis are always fresh and restorative, and this modern version using flowering vegetables is no different. You'll love the crisp crunch of this cooling pickle. You can use this brine for other hard vegetables as well – try carrots, Brussels sprouts and even asparagus.*

**Makes about a 2.3 litre (3¾ pint) jar**

100g (3½oz) salt

150g (5oz) broccoli, broken into small florets with stems removed and sliced into 5mm (¼in) pieces

150g (5oz) romanesco, broken into small florets with stems removed and sliced into 5mm (¼in) pieces

300g (11oz) cauliflower, broken into small florets with stems removed and sliced into 5mm (¼in) pieces

100g (3½oz) mu (Korean white radish) or mooli, peeled, cut into about 2.5cm (1in) thick discs. Cut each disc into 3 pieces lengthways, and then cut 5mm (¼in) slices across to make about 2.5cm (1in) squares

1 tsp garlic, grated or finely chopped

½ tsp ginger, grated or finely chopped

1 red chilli, thinly sliced at an angle

50g (2oz) white sugar

2 tbsp gochugaru (Korean chilli flakes)

In a large bowl, stir the salt into 1 litre (35fl oz) water until the salt has dissolved. Add the broccoli, romanesco, cauliflower and mu to the bowl. Leave at room temperature for 1 hour, then drain and save the liquid.

Toss the broccoli, romanesco, cauliflower and mu with the garlic, ginger and chopped red chilli and set aside.

In a large bowl, put 1 litre (35fl oz) of fresh water, 300ml (10fl oz) of the saved liquid, the sugar and gochugaru, and stir well. Filter this liquid through a piece of muslin, squeezing the muslin several times until the water turns a light red colour. Remove and discard the muslin and its contents.

Pour the gochugaru-infused water over the vegetables and stir well. Transfer to a clean glass jar or other non-reactive container. Cover and leave it to ferment at room temperature for about 16 hours. Refrigerate until ready to serve.

# Cabbage Kimchi with Oysters
## Gul Kimchi

*I love raw oysters and mixing them in with kimchi makes this ubiquitous side dish so luxurious. Adding fresh seafood, such as squid, scallops or raw oysters to kimchi is common and adds a deep umami flavour. Just make sure that the oysters are all submerged in the kimchi juices to ensure that they are covered with lactobacillum which protects the oysters, keeping them safe to eat.*

**Makes about 4.5 litres (8 Pints)**

230g (8oz) coarse sea salt

1 very large Korean cabbage or several heads Chinese cabbage (2.2–2.7kg/5–6lb total), bottom(s) trimmed, wilted or tough outer leaves discarded, and rinsed well

20 raw oysters, shucked and free of any bits of shell

3 carrots, julienned

12 wild chives, cut into 5cm (2in) pieces

200g (7oz) mu (Korean white radish) or mooli, peeled and julienned

ANCHOVY STOCK

2 small onions, roughly chopped

12 dried shiitake mushrooms

10 myulchi (large dried anchovies), heads and guts removed

6 spring onions, roughly chopped

8 garlic cloves, crushed

25cm (10in) piece of dashima (dried kelp)

SPICE PASTE

56 garlic cloves

250g (9oz) gochugaru (Korean chilli flakes)

14 tbsp fish sauce

10 tbsp salted shrimp, rinsed

4 tbsp white sugar

18cm (7in) piece of ginger, peeled and chopped

In a large bowl, stir together 2 litres (3 pints) warm water and 115g (4oz) of the salt until the salt has dissolved. Leave the salted water to cool.

Meanwhile, partially cut the cabbage in half lengthways, starting from the root end and cutting about halfway to the top. Using your hands, pull the cabbage apart to split in half completely. Repeat so that each half is halved in the same way, which keeps the leaves intact and whole.

Loosen the leaves of each wedge so that they are easy to spread. Sprinkle the remaining 115g (4oz) salt over and between all the leaves, salting the core area more heavily. Put the cabbage into a large bowl (use two if they don't fit) cut-side up. Pour the cooled salted water over the cabbage, then pour enough cold water into the bowl to cover the cabbage; don't overfill the bowl, as some liquid will be drawn out of the cabbage. Weigh down the cabbage with a plate so the wedges are completely immersed. Leave at room temperature for 6–8 hours, flipping the wedges halfway through.

Rinse the wedges well under cold running water and gently squeeze out any excess moisture. Put the wedges, cut-side down, in a colander and leave to drain for at least 30 minutes.

Meanwhile, make the anchovy stock. In a small saucepan, combine the onions, mushrooms, myulchi, spring onions, the

crushed garlic and dashima with 500ml (17fl oz) water and bring to
the boil over a high heat. Reduce the heat to maintain a simmer for
20 minutes. Strain the liquid, discarding the solids, and leave the
anchovy stock to cool completely.

Once the stock has cooled. Make the spice paste. Combine the
remaining garlic cloves, gochugaru, fish sauce, salted shrimp, sugar and
ginger in a food processor and process until smooth. Add enough of the
anchovy stock to make a smooth paste, about 475ml (16fl oz). Reserve
the remaining stock for soup or another dish. Transfer the spice paste
to a large bowl and stir in the oysters, carrots, wild chives and mu.

Rub the spice paste all over the cabbage wedges and between each
leaf. Pull the outermost leaf of each wedge tightly over the rest of the
wedge, forming a tidy parcel. Pack the wedges and oysters, carrots,
chives and mu into one or more glass or other non-reactive containers
with a tight-fitting lid (see Tip, below). Press a piece of clingfilm
directly on the surface of the kimchi, then cover.

The kimchi can be eaten at this young stage, or leave it to sit at room
temperature for about 2–3 days until it starts to get sour and 'bubble'
(the optimum temperature for fermentation is 65°C/18°F). Store the
kimchi in the fridge, where it will continue to ferment at a slower pace.
I like to age mine for at least 2 weeks, but it really is up to you.
Cut the kimchi before serving.

TIP
While large glass jars or Korean earthenware containers are preferred for
storing kimchi, they're not always easy to find. Look in the housewares
section of Asian markets for glass or plastic kimchi containers, which have
become popular. You can also use any sturdy BPA-free plastic or other
non-reactive container with a tight-fitting lid. You'll need a container or
containers with a total capacity of 4.5 litres (8 pints) for the kimchi.

# Korean Pickled Onion

## Yangpa Jangajji

*This pickled onion recipe is an old-time favourite and you'll quickly realise why. The addition of soy sauce to a traditional pickling liquid makes for an addictive umami-filled bite. This is one of my chefs', Mi Kyung Jeong's, recipes and she incorporates a bit of fresh chilli to add a little kick.*

500 g (1lb 2oz) large white onion, peeled and cut into 2.5cm (1in) dice
250 g (9oz) cucumber, deseeded and cut into 1cm (½in) thick half moons
200 g (7oz) celery, trimmed and sliced at an angle into 2cm (¾in) thick pieces
1 red chilli, sliced at an angle into 1cm (½in) thick pieces
1 green chilli, sliced at an angle into 1cm (½in) thick pieces

PICKLING LIQUID
250ml (8fl oz) soy sauce
185g (6½oz) white sugar
2½ tbsp soju (Korean spirit)
¼ tsp whole peppercorns
2–3 bay leaves
220ml (7¼fl oz) rice wine vinegar

Makes a 2 litre (1¾ pint) jar

Combine the onion, cucumber, celery and chillis in a large bowl and mix together. Place the mixed vegetables in a glass jar or an airtight container and set aside.

To make the pickling liquid, in a saucepan, put the the soy sauce, sugar, soju, peppercorns, bay leaves and 250ml (8fl oz) water and bring to the boil. Remove from the heat and add the vinegar.

Pour the hot pickling liquid into the jar, directly onto the vegetables.

Cover tightly and leave the pickle at room temperature overnight. Refrigerate for 3–4 days before serving

# Spicy Pickled Radishes

## Musaengchae

*This light and super fast pickle is very popular and a cinch to make. Its delectable tang and spice make it so incredibly yummy and goes particularly well with barbecue meat.*

600g (1lb 5oz) mu (Korean white radish) or mooli, peeled and julienned
4 tbsp sagwa-shikcho (Korean apple vinegar) or rice wine vinegar
6 tbsp white sugar
4 tbsp gochugaru (Korean chilli flakes)
4 tsp sea salt, or to taste

Makes a 500ml (17fl oz) jar

In a medium bowl, stir together all the ingredients until the mu is coated. Cover and refrigerate for about 1 hour, mixing well half way through. Check seasoning and adjust as necessary before serving.

# Spiced Pickled Green Papaya and Cucumber

*I am in love with the Thai green papaya dish, som tam, and I am known to eat platefuls of this tangy sweet and sour dish. This pickle is reminiscent of the Thai dish, and can be served either as a side dish or as a salad.*

**Makes a 2 litre (1¾ pint) jar**

450g (1lb) green papaya, peeled and julienned into long strips
150g (5oz) cucumber, cut into quarters lengthways, deseeded and sliced at an angle into 1cm (½in) thick slices
2 tbsp sagwa-shikcho (Korean apple vinegar) or rice wine vinegar
2 tbsp white sugar
3 tbsp gochugaru (Korean chilli flakes), or to taste
½ garlic clove, grated
2 tsp salt

Place the papaya and cucumber in a large bowl; set aside.

In a small bowl, whisk together the vinegar, sugar, gochugaru, garlic and salt until the sugar is dissolved. Tip the dressing into the bowl with the papaya and cucumber and toss until well coated.

Cover and refrigerate for about 1 hour before serving.

# Cucumber and Yuja Pickle

*At my restaurant, we make this popular pickle by the bucketful. The addition of yuja or yuzu juice makes for the most delightfully fragrant pickle; it tastes special and the look of surprise you'll see on your guests' faces upon first bite will assure you that this recipe is a keeper.*

**Makes a 2 litre (1¾ pint) jar**

1kg (2lb 4oz) Asian cucumbers, deseeded and sliced into 1cm (½in) thick half moons
500ml (17fl oz) yuja (yuzu) juice
160ml (5½fl oz) sagwa-shikcho (Korean apple vinegar)
325g (11½ oz) white sugar

Place the cucumbers in a glass jar or an airtight container; set aside.

In a medium bowl, combine the yuja juice, vinegar and sugar and whisk together until the sugar is dissolved. Pour the liquid into the jar, directly onto the mixture and stir. Press a piece of clingfilm directly onto the surface of the cucumber, then cover with the lid. Refrigerate for a day to allow to pickle before serving.

# DUMPLINGS

Every culture has some form of pastry
wrapped around a filling. In Korea, we
have dumplings, mandoo, that hide all
kinds of delightful treasures inside.
This chapter has traditional and modern
fusion recipes that will please every palate.

# Philly Cheesesteak Dumplings

*At my restaurant, we sell these dumplings as fast as we can make them. There is something so incredibly delicious about the combination of galbi beef, kimchi and cheese, mixed with some pickled jalapeño – it is a recipe to please, and a great snack alongside ice-cold beers.*

**Makes about 45 dumplings**

50 thin square eggless wonton wrappers 10cm (4in)
vegetable oil, for frying

FILLING
150g (5oz) shiitake mushrooms, stems removed and finely chopped
1 tbsp roasted sesame oil
500g (1lb 2oz) cooked meat from the Grilled Beef Short Ribs (page 129)
300g (11oz) cabbage kimchi, finely chopped
100g (3½oz) spring onions, finely chopped
75g (3oz) pickled jalapeños, finely chopped
500g (1lb 2oz) mature Cheddar cheese, grated
sea salt and freshly ground black pepper, to taste

TO SERVE
silgochu (dried chilli threads)
1 spring onion, julienned and soaked in iced water until curled, then drained
Sriracha

For the filling, first sauté the mushrooms in the sesame oil in a large non-stick frying pan over medium–low heat until just softened. Remove from the heat and set aside. In a large bowl, combine the rest of the filling ingredients with the mushrooms. Mix together using your hands, really breaking up the short rib meat to make a uniform texture.

For the dumplings, line a couple of baking sheets with parchment and set aside. Fill a small bowl with water. Unwrap the wonton wrappers and cover lightly with a piece of clingfilm to keep them moist. Lay a wrapper on a clean work surface and put 25g (1oz) of the meat filling in the centre. Dip a forefinger into the water and run it along the edges of the wrapper to moisten the surface. Now bring the open edges to the centre, and pinch where the edges meet each other, creating four seams in a cross shape. Set aside and cover with clingfilm or a damp tea towel while you shape the rest. Repeat with the remaining wrappers and filling, making sure the dumplings are not touching on the baking sheets.

To a medium saucepan, add the vegetable oil and heat to 170°C (340°F). Working in batches, place the dumplings on their sides in the pan in a single layer without crowding. Cook for 3–4 minutes until golden brown. Transfer the fried dumplings to a wire rack or kitchen paper-lined plate to drain. Repeat with the remaining dumplings. If you don't plan on cooking them straight away, you can freeze them on the baking sheets, then bag them up and store in the freezer.

Top with some of the silgochu and curly spring onion and serve immediately with the Sriracha.

# Pork and Kimchi Dumplings

*I have such strong memories of making dumplings with my whole family as a child. Pork and kimchi go so well together and the addition of a little bacon makes the flavour pop even more. You can leave the tofu out, if you like, but I find that it really helps keep the dumplings moist and juicy. These little parcels freeze beautifully too; line them up on trays, freeze, then place in containers or a bag for easy cooking later. Add a couple to a bowl of soup to make it a meal, or serve as an afternoon snack, or an easy crowd-pleasing appetizer.*

**Makes 45 dumplings**

50 thin, round eggless wonton wrappers,
   10cm (4in) diameter

FILLING
400g (14oz) pork mince
150g (5oz) streaky bacon, very finely
   chopped
100g (3½oz) firm tofu, drained and crumbled
100g (3½oz) cabbage kimchi, chopped and
   drained
200g (7oz) dangmyun (sweet potato
   noodles), cooked according to the packet
   instructions, drained and roughly chopped
2 tsp soy sauce
2 tsp roasted sesame oil
2 tsp roasted sesame seeds, semi-crushed
1 garlic clove, grated or finely chopped
1 tsp ginger, peeled and grated
1 tsp fine sea salt
¼ tsp black pepper, freshly ground
2 spring onions, chopped

TO SERVE
red chilli, thinly sliced at an angle
handful of chives, cut into 3cm (1¼in) lengths
black sesame seeds
Chilli-Soy Dipping Sauce (page 14)

TIP
If you'd like to check the seasoning of the
filling for the dumplings – or any kind of filling
or stuffing that includes raw meat or fish –
cook a small patty in a lightly oiled pan, taste,
then adjust the seasonings to your taste.

In a large bowl, combine the filling ingredients. Mix together using your hands, really breaking up the tofu to make a uniform texture.

Line a couple of baking sheets with parchment and set aside. Fill a small bowl with water. Unwrap the wonton wrappers and cover lightly with a piece of clingfilm to keep them from drying out. Lay a wrapper on a clean work surface and spoon about 25g (1oz) of the meat filling into the centre. Dip a forefinger into the water and run it along the edges of the wrapper to moisten the surface. Fold the wrapper in half. Starting at the top of the half-circle and working towards the ends, press firmly together to seal, pressing out any air bubbles. Pleat from one corner to the other ends, gather the pleat at the top and pinch them all together to make pomegranate shape.

Lay the dumpling on its side on one of the prepared baking sheets. Repeat with the remaining wrappers and filling, making sure the dumplings are not touching on the baking sheets.

Once the dumplings are assembled, place them in a prepared steamer basket, working in batches if necessary and leaving at least 2.5cm (1 in) of space between each one, as they will expand when cooking. Steam the dumplings until cooked through, for about 8 minutes, then transfer to a serving platter. Or cook as you please: pan fry, boil or deep fry. If you don't plan to cook them straight away, you can freeze them on the baking sheets, then bag them up to store in the freezer.

Sprinkle with the chilli, chives and black sesame seeds and serve immediately with the dipping sauce.

# Scallop and Tobiko Dumplings

*I am a huge seafood lover and fresh scallops are such a special treat. When I was working in restaurants in my early days, I used to have to scrape the scallops out of the shells every morning. I still remember the smell of the sea, when opening the box. In this recipe, I let the sweetness of the scallops shine through with just a hint of wasabi, and the fresh tobiko to finish brings your tastebuds back to the sea.*

**Makes about 45 dumplings**

50 thin, square eggless wonton wrappers 10cm (4in)
vegetable oil, for frying

FILLING
950g (2lb 2oz) scallops, cleaned, trimmed and cut into 1cm (½in) pieces
1 tsp garlic, grated or finely chopped
4 tsp ginger, peeled and grated
2 tbsp chives, finely chopped
2 tbsp roasted sesame seeds, crushed
3 tbsp wasabi paste
2½ tbsp roasted sesame oil
1 tsp salt

TO SERVE
100g (3½oz) red tobiko (flying fish roe)
Chilli-Soy Dipping Sauce (page 14)

For the filling, in a large bowl, combine all of the filling ingredients until the wasabi has been fully incorporated.

For the dumplings, place a wrapper on a flat surface and add 25g (1oz) of the filling to the bottom third of the wrapper. Using your finger, wet the edges and fold the bottom edge upwards, closing the side edges and seal shut once reaching the top to create a pillow shape. Repeat to use all the wrappers and filling, covering the finished dumplings with clingfilm to prevent them from drying out.

In a large frying pan, heat about 1 tablespoon vegetable oil over a medium–high heat.

Working in batches, lay the dumplings, sealed side down, in the pan in a single layer without crowding the pan. Cook for 2–3 minutes until golden brown on the base. Flip them and cook for a further 2–3 minutes until golden brown and the filling is cooked through. Transfer the fried dumplings to a wire rack or kitchen paper-lined plate to drain. Repeat with the remaining dumplings, adding more oil to the pan as needed. If you prefer not to fry the dumplings, steam them in batches until cooked through, about 6 minutes, then transfer to a serving platter (steamed dumplings do not need to be drained).

Transfer the fried dumplings to a platter. Top with some of the tobiko and serve immediately with the dipping sauce.

# Wild Mushroom and Truffle Dumplings

*This luxurious fusion mandoo has been one of the most popular dumplings on the menu at my restaurants. The mushroom duxelle goes beautifully well with dwengjang, heightening the umami hits on all levels. Vegetarians and meat eaters alike love this little bundle of flavour.*

**Makes about 45 dumplings**

50 thin, round eggless wonton wrappers, 10cm (4in) diameter

HERB OIL
100ml (3½fl oz) extra virgin olive oil
10g (¼oz) thyme, washed and dried
10g (¼oz) oregano, washed and dried
10g (¼oz) rosemary, washed and dried

TRUFFLE DIPPING SAUCE
180ml (6¼fl oz) soy sauce
1 tbsp black truffle paste
3 tbsp black truffle oil
2½ tbsp lemon juice
2 tbsp yuja (yuzu) juice
2 tbsp mirin
2 tsp rice wine vinegar
2½ tsp caster sugar

FILLING
2 garlic cloves, grated or finely chopped
½ small onion, finely diced
350g (12oz) shiitake mushrooms, stems removed and roughly sliced
350g (12oz) shimeji mushrooms, stems removed and roughly sliced
350g (12oz) portobello mushrooms, caps peeled, stems removed and roughly sliced
85g (3oz) dwengjang (Korean soy bean paste)
85g (3oz) unsalted butter, at room temperature
2 tsp porcini powder
40g (1½oz) black truffle paste
35g (1¼oz) chives, finely chopped
sea salt and freshly ground black pepper

For the herb oil, in a medium deep pan, slowly and gently heat the olive oil and add the herbs. Remove from the heat and leave it to steep for 30 minutes. (The longer the oil sits with the herbs, the stronger the flavour will be.) Meanwhile, to make the truffle dipping sauce, whisk together all the ingredients in a small bowl.

Remove the herbs from the steeping oil then heat the oil over a medium heat. Add the garlic and onion and cook until softened, stirring often. Add the mushrooms and dwengjang and cook, stirring occasionally, for 15–20 minutes, or until the mixture becomes dry. Remove from the heat and stir in the soft butter. Chop the mushroom mixture into small pieces using a food processor (or by hand into 5mm/¼in pieces). Set aside to cool, then add the porcini powder, truffle paste and chives and mix well. Season with salt and pepper.

For the dumplings, fill a small bowl with water. Working with one wrapper at a time on a clean surface, spoon 25g (1oz) of the filling into the centre of the wrapper. Dip a forefinger in the water and run it along the edges of the wrapper to moisten. Fold the wrapper in half away from you. Starting at the top of the half circle and working towards the ends, press firmly together to seal, pressing out any air bubbles. Take the pointy ends of the half circle and pull them together, folding them downwards and towards each other so they overlap slightly and form a shape that resembles a nurse's cap. Dab the place where the ends meet with a little water and pinch together to seal. Lay the dumplings in a steamer basket, leaving at least 2.5cm (1in) of space between the dumplings, as they will expand when cooked. (Cook the dumplings in batches, if needed.)

To cook, bring the water in the steamer base to a steady simmer. Set the steamer basket over the water, cover and steam the dumplings for 7 minutes, or until cooked through. Repeat with the remaining dumplings, if needed. Serve immediately with the dipping sauce.

# Fish and Mushy Beans

## with kimchi tartare sauce

*I have been living in the UK for over a decade and have grown to love 'fish and chips'.
This is my Korean version in the form of a dumpling. The lemon and miso marinade
gives the halibut a nice savoury tang and the kimchi tartare sauce is so delicious,
you won't be able to go back to regular tartare sauce.*

**Makes about 35 dumplings**

50 thin, round eggless wonton wrappers,
  10cm (4in) diameter
2 egg yolks, beaten
150g (5oz) panko breadcrumbs
vegetable oil, for frying

FILLING
3 tbsp extra virgin olive oil
2 tsp chicken stock
1 tsp garlic, grated or finely chopped
40g (1½oz) white miso
550g (1lb 4oz) halibut, boneless and
  skinless, chopped into 1cm (½in) pieces
grated zest of 1 lemon
200g (7oz) frozen edamame beans
2 tbsp butter
75ml (3fl oz) double cream
50g (2oz) Parmesan, finely grated
sea salt and freshly ground black pepper
bonito flakes, to serve

KIMCHI TARTARE SAUCE
100g (3½oz) Kewpie mayonnaise
25g (1oz) cabbage kimchi, finely
  chopped
1 tbsp parsley, finely chopped
2 tsp lemon juice
1 tsp Dijon mustard
½ tsp Worcestershire sauce

First, make the filling. In a small bowl, whisk together the olive oil, chicken stock, garlic and miso. Place the halibut in a plastic bag and pour in the mixture. Add the lemon zest and salt and pepper to taste and place in the fridge to marinate for at least 30 minutes and up to 8 hours.

To make the tartare sauce, mix all of the ingredients together in a small bowl. Cover and chill until ready to use.

Cook the edamame beans according to the directions on the bag. Remove the skins. Place in a food processor and pulse a few times to start breaking down the beans. Add the butter, cream and Parmesan, then blend until it's relatively smooth, but still a little chunky. Place in a bowl and set aside.

In a large, non stick frying pan, cook the halibut for 1–2 minutes, until roughly half cooked. Place in a colander to drain the liquid and oil. In a large bowl, mix together the drained halibut and the edamame purée and season well with salt and pepper.

Lay a wrapper on a clean work surface and spoon about 25g (1oz) of the filling into the centre. Fill a small bowl with water, wet a finger and run it along the edges of the wrapper then fold in half to make a crescent shape. Brush the outer side of each of the dumplings with egg wash and roll in the panko breadcrumbs.

Half fill a medium-sized saucepan with oil and heat to 170°C (340°F) using a thermometer. Deep fry the dumplings for about 4 minutes until golden brown. Serve the dumplings with the tartare sauce.

# Brown Shrimp and Broccoli Dumplings

*I never really ate brown shrimps until I arrived in the UK, and they quickly became an addiction. These mini crustaceans add a ton of shrimp flavour, making these prawn and shrimp dumplings so delectable.*

**Makes about 45 dumplings**

50 thin, round eggless wonton wrappers, 10cm (4in) diameter

FILLING
2 tbsp butter
250g (9oz) broccoli, chopped into small pieces
1 tsp garlic, grated or finely chopped
½ tsp ginger, peeled and grated
260g (9¼oz) brown shrimp
200g (7oz) tiger prawns, cleaned, deshelled, deveined and roughly chopped
340g (11½oz) tiger prawns, cleaned deshelled, deveined and puréed using a food processor
4 spring onions, finely chopped
2 tsp roasted sesame seeds, crushed
2 tbsp roasted sesame oil
½ tsp white sugar
2 tsp fine sea salt
7 twists of the black pepper mill
Chilli-Soy Dipping Sauce (page 14), to serve

For the filling, heat the butter in a large non-stick frying pan over a medium heat. Add the broccoli, garlic, ginger and a pinch of salt and cook for about 2 minutes, stirring frequently until the broccoli is softened. Remove from the heat and transfer to a medium bowl. Add the rest of the filling ingredients to the bowl and mix together well using your hands.

For the dumplings, line two baking sheets with parchment and set aside. Fill a small bowl with water. Unwrap the wonton wrappers and cover lightly with a piece of clingfilm to keep them from drying out. Lay a wrapper on a clean work surface and put 25g (1oz) of the filling in the centre. Fold the bottom edge upwards, closing the side edges and seal shut once reaching the top to create a pillow shape. Repeat to use all the wrappers and filling, covering the finished dumplings with clingfilm to prevent them from drying out.

Steam the dumplings for 9 minutes, or until cooked through.

Serve immediately with the dipping sauce.

# Chicken with Ginger and Shiitake Mushroom Dumplings

*This fragrant ginger-infused chicken dumpling is light and satisfying. The earthy, nutty hint of sesame oil blends amazingly well with the shiitake mushrooms. Do make sure you add enough fresh black pepper, as the subtle heat brings a nice peppery warmth to this tasty pillowy bite.*

**Makes about 45 dumplings**

50 thin, round eggless wonton wrappers, 10cm (4in) diameter
vegetable oil, for sautéing
Chilli-Soy Dipping Sauce (page 14), to serve

FILLING

300g (11oz) shiitake mushrooms, stems removed and cut into 5mm (¼in) dice
100g (3½oz) Chinese cabbage, cut into 5mm (¼in) squared pieces
a large pinch of salt
700g (1lb 9oz) chicken thighs, finely chopped
50g (2oz) chives, finely chopped
2 tsp ginger, peeled and grated
1 tsp garlic, grated or finely chopped
2 tsp white sugar
2 tsp roasted sesame seeds, semi crushed
4 tsp roasted sesame oil
1 tsp fine sea salt
4 tsp soy sauce
20 twists of the black pepper mill

For the filling, heat a large non-stick frying pan drizzled with oil over a medium-high heat. Add the mushrooms, cabbage and salt. Cook while continuously stirring for a few minutes until the mushroom and cabbage are just softened and the liquid has evaporated. Remove from the heat and transfer to a medium bowl. Add the rest of the filling ingredients to the bowl and mix together using your hands.

For the dumplings, line two baking sheets with parchment and set aside. Fill a small bowl with water. Unwrap the wonton wrappers and cover lightly with a piece of clingfilm to keep them from drying out. Lay a wrapper on a clean work surface and put 25g (1oz) of the filling in the centre. Fold the bottom edge upwards, closing the side edges and seal shut once reaching the top to create a pillow shape. Repeat to use all the wrappers and filling, covering the finished dumplings with clingfilm to prevent them from drying out.

Steam the dumplings for 9 minutes, or until cooked through.

Serve immediately with the dipping sauce.

# STREET FOOD

Korean street food is dynamic and full of the wonderful and wacky. I'm always discovering new trends on the pavements, and indulging in old favourites. Fried food on sticks is forever popular to eat on the go, as well as savoury pancakes that are the perfect after-work snack with a beer.

# Seafood Pancakes

## Haemul Pajeon

*These pancakes, boasting treasures from the sea, are one of Korea's most popular appetizers. You can substitute any shellfish here, but you'll find that the combination of brown shrimp, mussels and clams pack these pancakes full of flavour without waterlogging them, keeping them crispy. The pancake dipping sauce I make to serve alongside is a little thicker than normal and full of spices, as I like it to 'stick' to the jeon and find its way into the nooks and crannies, adding more flavour.*

**Makes 4–5 pancakes**

50g (2oz) mussels, cleaned and debearded
50g (2oz) clams, cleaned
95g (3¼oz) rice flour
2 tbsp cornflour
65g (2½oz) self-raising flour
2 tbsp dwengjang (Korean soy bean paste)
¼ tsp ground black pepper
3 large pinches of sea salt
100g (3½oz) brown shrimp
5 spring onions, julienned
1 tsp garlic, grated or finely chopped
2 red chillies, thinly sliced at an angle
vegetable oil, for frying
Pancake Dipping Sauce (page 14), to serve

In a large saucepan, add enough water so that it's three-quarters full and bring to the boil. Add the mussels and clams and cook until the shells open. Remove the shellfish and set aside to cool. Retain 20g (¾oz) of the cooking liquor then strain it to remove any pieces of shell or grit. Once cool enough to touch, remove the meat from the shells of the mussels and clams and set aside.

In a large bowl, gently whisk together the rice flour, cornflour, self-raising flour, dwengjang, pepper, salt and 220g (8oz) of cold water and liquor from the cooked shellfish until smooth. Add the brown shrimp, mussels, clams, spring onions, garlic and red chillies (keeping the seeds, if you like more heat), and stir the batter until thoroughly combined.

In a large non-stick frying pan, heat 3 tablespoons of oil over a medium–high heat. Spoon in the batter and spread it evenly to form a pancake about 12cm (5in) wide. Fry until golden brown and crispy on the base, about 3–4 minutes.

Carefully flip and cook for a further 3–4 minutes until the other side is golden. Transfer to a kitchen paper-lined plate to drain. Repeat with the remaining batter, adding more oil to the frying pan as needed.

Serve immediately with the pancake dipping sauce.

# Saewoo Prawn Pops Balls

*I developed these light prawn balls inspired by the many items served on sticks I have seen in Seoul. We launched my restaurant with these on the menu and they quickly became a signature item. Just a few bites of heaven on a stick!*

**Makes 15 pops**

55g (2oz) plain flour
2 eggs
100g (3½oz) panko breadcrumbs
vegetable oil, for frying

FILLING
400g (14oz) prawns, cleaned, deshelled
  and deveined
1 large egg, lightly beaten
1 spring onion, finely chopped
30g (1oz) panko breadcrumbs
1 tbsp Dijon mustard
1 tsp lemon juice
1 tbsp Sriracha
Gochujang Mayonnaise (page 14),
  to serve

First make the filling. In a food processor fitted with an S-shape blade, finely chop half of the prawns. Hand chop the other half of the prawns into chunkier pieces. Transfer all the prawns to a bowl and add the rest of the filling ingredients. Gently mix using your hands until evenly incorporated.

Line a couple of baking sheets with parchment and set aside. Form the mix into small balls – around 30g (1oz) each – and lay them on the prepared baking sheets, making sure the balls are not touching each other. Freeze them on the baking sheets until hard.

To coat the balls, set up three dipping stations: spread out the flour on a dinner plate; use a fork to whisk 2 eggs in a small, wide bowl; and pour the panko breadcrumbs onto another dinner plate. Without thawing the frozen prawn balls, coat one with the flour, shaking it to remove the excess, then with the egg wash and lastly with the panko, making sure it is well covered. Repeat to coat all the balls.

Into a large, heavy-based pan at least 13cm (5in) deep, pour the oil to a depth of 5cm (2in) and heat over a medium–high heat to 170°C (340°F). Working in two batches, fry the coated balls for 4–5 minutes until golden brown and cooked through. Transfer to a kitchen paper-lined plate to drain. Let the oil return to temperature before cooking the second batch. Serve the prawn pops with gochujang mayonnaise on the side.

# Garlic Chive Pancake

## Buchu Jeon

*My friend Jean took me to a small restaurant in Seoul that serves up the best buchu jeon. It is best to go when garlic chives are in season and at their sweetest. The chives cook down to almost nothing so don't be alarmed by the volume at first. I guarantee that this pancake will be devoured immediately once at the table.*

**Makes 1 large pancake (serves 4–6)**

95g (3¼oz) rice flour
2 tbsp cornflour
65g (2½oz) self-raising flour
2 tbsp dwengjang (Korean soy bean paste)
¼ tsp ground black pepper
3 large pinches of sea salt
vegetable oil, for frying
350g (12oz) garlic chives, cut into 5cm (2in) lengths
Pancake Dipping Sauce (page 14), to serve

In a large bowl, gently whisk together the rice flour, cornflour, self-raising flour, dwengjang, pepper, salt and 315ml (11fl oz) cold water until smooth.

Place a large non-stick frying pan over a medium–low heat and drizzle with oil. Place a handful of chives in the pan and pour in just enough batter to make a thin pancake, coating the top of the chives, too. Cook for about 2–3 minutes until crispy, then flip carefully and cook for another 2–3 minutes until the chives are wilted and the pancake is golden. Remove from the heat and place on a kitchen paper-lined plate. Keep it in warm place.

To serve, cut the pancake into wedges and serve immediately with pancake dipping sauce

# Pan-fried Korean Courgette Fritters

## Hobak Jeon

*Korean courgettes are so much tastier than their Western counterparts. Yellow in hue,
sweeter and denser, they are well worth hunting down. I can eat these by the dozen,
and they remind me of the much-loved, thinly-sliced Italian courgette fries.*

**Serves 4–6**

60g (2½oz) rice flour
3 eggs, beaten
2 small hobak (Korean courgettes)
  or regular courgettes, cut into 1cm
  (½in) slices
vegetable oil, for frying
1 Korean red chilli or Fresno chilli, sliced
  into 2.5–5cm (1–2in) lengths (optional)
handful of chives, sliced into 2.5–5cm
  (1–2in) lengths (optional)
sea salt and freshly ground black pepper
Pancake Dipping Sauce (page 14),
  to serve

Put the flour and beaten eggs into separate wide, shallow bowls.
Spread the courgette slices out in a single layer on a baking sheet.
Season lightly with salt and pepper and set aside for about 5 minutes
so the seasonings soak in a bit.

Lightly dredge each courgette slice in the flour, tapping off any excess.

In a large non-stick frying pan, heat a good drizzle of oil over a
medium heat. Working in batches, coat the courgette slices in egg,
letting any excess drip into the bowl, and place into the frying pan.
If desired, press chillies and chives into the surface of the batter. Cook
for about 3 minutes, until golden on the bottom, then flip the slices
over and cook the other side for the same amount of time. Transfer to
a wire rack or kitchen paper-lined plate to drain. Keep warm while you
cook the next batch, adding more oil to the pan if needed.

Transfer to a platter and serve immediately with the dipping sauce.

# Kimchi Arancini

*Arancini is a fantastic way to use leftover rice, transforming it into an appetizer that flies off the plate. You can use any kind of old rice, but short grain works best.*

**Makes 25 balls**

500g (1lb 2oz) steamed short grain rice, chilled

150g (5oz) cabbage kimchi, finely chopped

50g (2oz) Parmesan, finely grated

a good pinch of kizami nori (roasted shredded seaweed)

2 tsp roasted sesame oil

2 spring onions, finely chopped

75g (3oz) Cheddar cheese, cut into 1cm (½in) dice

55g (2oz) plain flour

2 eggs

100g (3½oz) panko breadcrumbs

vegetable oil, for frying

sea salt and freshly ground black pepper

Sriracha, to serve

SWEET SOY SAUCE

125ml (4fl oz) soy sauce

1 tbsp rice wine vinegar

2 tbsp mirin

50g dark brown sugar

1 large clove garlic, grated

½ tsp ginger, grated

½ tsp gochugaru (Korean chilli flakes)

½ tsp roasted sesame oil

½ tsp cornflour

First, make the sweet soy sauce. Heat the soy sauce, rice wine vinegar, mirin, dark brown sugar, garlic, ginger, gochugaru and sesame oil in a small saucepan over a medium heat and whisk well until the sugar has dissolved. Set aside 3½ teaspoons and then store the remainder of the sauce in the fridge to enjoy with Korean fried chicken or another recipe.

Mix the cornflour with 2 tablespoons of water and whisk into the sweet soy sauce. Bring the sauce to the boil and remove from the heat. Pass through fine sieve and set aside.

Place the chilled cooked rice into a large bowl, add the kimchi, Parmesan, kizami nori, sesame oil, soy sauce and spring onions, and mix together well. Season with salt and pepper to taste.

Roll the mix into balls about 20g (¾oz) each, and place a dice of cheese into the middle of each ball. Place the balls on a lined baking sheet and place in the refrigerator. Chill until hard, about 2–3 hours.

To coat the arancini, set up three dipping stations: spread out the flour on a dinner plate; use a fork to whisk the eggs in a small, wide bowl; and pour the panko on to another dinner plate. Coat one of the balls with the flour, shaking it to remove the excess, then with the egg wash and lastly with the panko, making sure it is well covered. Repeat to coat all the arancini.

In a large, heavy-based pan at least 13cm (5in) deep, pour oil to a depth of 5cm (2in) and heat over a medium–high heat to 170°C (340°F). Working in batches, fry the coated balls for 4–5 minutes until golden brown and cooked through. Transfer to a kitchen paper-lined plate to drain. Let the oil return to temperature before cooking the next batch, keeping previous batches warm in a low heated oven.

Serve the arancini immediately with Sriracha on the side.

# Spring Vegetable Twigim

## Yachae Twigim

*Twigim is the Korean version of tempura. Here, I am using spring vegetables, as the colours come through so nicely. Feel free to experiment and use other unusual veggies and leaves, such as kohlrabi, kale and perilla leaves.*

**Serves 2–4**

5 stems purple sprouting broccoli, bottoms
    trimmed
12 sugar snap peas
8 baby stem asparagus, bottoms trimmed
5 baby corn
5 rainbow baby carrots, peeled and trimmed
½ fennel bulb, sliced into 2.5mm (⅛in)
    thick pieces
3 baby leeks, cut in half lengthways
5 oyster mushrooms
2 Jerusalem artichokes, peeled and sliced
    into 2.5mm (⅛in) thick pieces at an angle
250g (9oz) tempura flour
360–400ml (12–14fl oz) soda water, cold
vegetable oil, for frying
Pancake Dipping Sauce (page 14), to serve

In a large bowl, toss the vegetables in the tempura flour to coat lightly. Remove the vegetables, shaking off the excess flour, and place on a rack.

For the batter, mix the tempura flour and soda water together in the bowl, adding the water slowly as you may not need all of it. Mix lightly with chopsticks, keeping the batter rather lumpy.

Half fill a heavy-based saucepan with oil and heat to 180°C (350°F). Working in batches, dip the vegetables into the batter to coat, then place them into the oil. Fry the vegetables for 3–4 minutes until they are cooked through and the batter is golden brown.

Remove the vegetables from the oil with a slotted spoon and place on a rack to drain, keeping warm. Repeat to coat and fry all the vegetables.

Serve the twigim immediately with the dipping sauce.

# Sweet Potato Pancake

## Goguma Jeon

*Sweet potatoes are so zeitgeist right now and showing up on menus everywhere. I love Korea's traditional potato pancakes, but decided to reinvent them here with the beloved sweet potato. The leeks add a great savoury quality, and the gochugaru lends some nice heat to balance the sweet spuds. Do sprinkle with pumpkin seeds to finish, as they add great texture and a welcome nuttiness.*

**Makes 12 small pancakes**

450g (1lb) sweet potatoes, or similar,
  peeled and roughly chopped
¼ small onion, roughly chopped
¼ leek, finely diced
2 tbsp potato starch
1 tbsp roasted sesame seeds, crushed
2 tsp gochugaru (Korean chilli flakes)
1 tsp gochujang (Korean chilli paste)
1 tsp fine sea salt
2 large eggs, lightly beaten
vegetable oil, for frying

TO SERVE
toasted pumpkin seeds
Pancake Dipping Sauce (page 14)

In a food processor fitted with a medium grating disc, shred the sweet potatoes and onion, alternating between the two (the onion juices keep the potatoes from discolouring). Alternatively, grate the potatoes and onion on the large holes of a box grater.

Transfer the mixture to a large bowl, add the leek, potato starch, sesame seeds, gochugaru, gochujang and salt and toss together. Add the beaten eggs and mix well.

In a large non-stick frying pan, heat 5mm (¼in) of oil over a medium heat. Working in batches, spoon tablespoons of the batter into the frying pan to form pancakes (1 tablespoon per pancake) about 7cm (3in) wide. Cook for about 3–4 minutes until golden brown on the base. Flip the pancakes over and press down firmly with the back of your spatula. Continue cooking for about 3 minutes until the other side is golden brown. Transfer to a wire rack or kitchen paper-lined plate to drain. Repeat with the remaining mixture, adding more oil to the pan as needed.

Serve the pancakes hot, sprinkled with toasted pumpkin seeds, with the pancake dipping sauce on the side.

# Deep-fried Baby Squid
## Korean Ojingeo Twigim

*On the streets of Seoul, you can often buy a huge whole squid on a stick and gnaw on it for hours. I have replicated this fun snack using baby squid, to make it a little more manageable to cook and tender to eat as well. You don't have to skewer these, if you don't want to, you can simply fry free-form for a bowl of light, crispy squid bites.*

**Makes 4 squid**

4 baby squid, cleaned
65g (2½oz) cornflour, plus extra for coating
20g (¾oz) fine matzo meal
30g (1oz) plain flour
2 tsp sea salt
⅛ tsp baking powder
90ml (3fl oz) vodka (or any neutral-tasting, 40% alcohol)
freshly ground black pepper
Gochujang Mayonnaise (page 14), to serve

Skewer the squid with bamboo skewers, weaving the bamboo through the squid to make it lay flat and secure (you may need to cut the skewers down). Make a cross, with a long skewer going up the base of the squid to the top and a shorter one going across the body from left to right to spread out the sides. Put some cornflour on a tray or dinner plate, add the squid and toss to coat, shaking each piece to remove any excess.

In a large, heavy-based pan at least 13cm (5in) deep, pour oil to a depth of 5cm (2in) and heat over a medium–high heat to 180°C (350°F).

While the oil is heating, in a large bowl, whisk together the 65g (2½oz) cornflour, matzo meal, flour, salt, baking powder and pepper for the batter. Just before frying the squid, whisk the vodka and 120ml (4fl oz) water into the cornflour mixture. Don't do this in advance or the resulting batter may thicken too much as it sits. The consistency should be relatively thin and runny.

Working in batches, dip the squid into the batter, letting any excess drip off. Suspend the squid in the oil for a couple of seconds to set the crust, before letting it slip completely into the oil; otherwise, it will stick to the base of the pan. Fry the squid for 5–8 minutes, flipping halfway through, until golden brown and cooked through. Transfer to a wire rack or kitchen paper-lined plate to drain. Let the oil return to 180°C (350°F) before cooking the second batch. Keep the cooked squid in a warm place and serve with gochujang mayonnaise.

# Dwengjang Lamb Scotch Egg

*Scotch eggs are the quintessential British gastropub snack, and recently I was served these at a cricket match. I was, admittedly, a little bored (has the game started yet?), so I studied my snack intently and devised a Korean version using lamb. The dwengjang marries well with the lamb, giving this Scotch egg a decidedly Korean edge.*

**Makes 8 Scotch eggs**

8 eggs
8 perilla leaves
2 eggs, beaten
100g (3½oz) plain flour, seasoned with
  salt and pepper
125g (4oz) panko breadcrumbs
vegetable oil, for deep frying

LAMB FILLING
400g (14oz) lamb mince
1 tbsp white miso
1 tbsp dwengjang (Korean soy
  bean paste)
1 tsp gochujang (Korean chilli paste)
¼ onion, grated
1 garlic clove, finely chopped
1 tsp sake
2 tsp mirin
1 tsp honey
1 tsp soy sauce
1 tsp roasted sesame oil
20g (¾oz) chives, chopped
40g (1½oz) panko breadcrumbs
sea salt and freshly ground black pepper
Gochujang Mayonnaise or Gochujang
  Mustard (page 14), to serve

Bring a medium pan of salted water to a rapid boil, then lower to a simmer, add the whole eggs to the pan and simmer for 5 minutes. Plunge the eggs into ice-cold water. Leave them to cool completely, then peel and set aside. These can be boiled the day before.

For the filling, place the lamb mince and the rest of the ingredients into a bowl, season and mix well with your hands. Divide the meat mixture into eight portions, place each portion between two pieces of clingfilm and roll into a flat round with a rolling pin, about 1cm (½in) thick. Place on a tray and chill in the fridge for 20 minutes.

To assemble, wrap a boiled egg with a perilla leaf, then place the egg in the centre of a meat round. Wrap the meat around the egg and roll into the shape of a ball. Repeat to cover all the eggs with meat.

Now, for the coating: roll each egg in the flour, shaking off the excess, then dip into the beaten egg and then roll in the panko breadcrumbs.

Half fill a heavy-based saucepan with oil and heat to 170°C (340°F). Deep fry two eggs at a time for 6–8 minutes until golden and crispy. Drain on kitchen paper, then serve with gochujang mayonnaise or gochujang mustard.

# Mushrooms Stuffed with Beef and Pork

*This recipe was inspired by a trip to Madrid, where I went to a restaurant that only served mushrooms and chorizo. A single chef stood at a solid-top grill lined with dozens of mushroom caps, each cradling a single piece of chorizo. The fat of the sausage would fill the cap with flavourful drippings while cooking, and the chef simply squeezed fresh lemon juice on top to serve. This version is reminiscent of a Korean jeon, while incorporating spicy chorizo and of course, finishing with a kiss of lemon.*

**Makes 15 mushrooms**

15 large shiitake mushrooms, cleaned and stems removed
100g (3½oz) cured chorizo, very finely diced
200g (7oz) beef mince
2 garlic cloves, grated
2 tbsp finely chopped parsley
1 spring onion, finely chopped
80g (3oz) plain flour
2 eggs
vegetable oil, for frying
1 lemon, cut into wedges
sea salt and freshly ground black pepper

Using a paring knife, score an 'X' on the top of each mushroom. Set aside.

In a large bowl, mix together the chorizo, beef mince, garlic, parsley, spring onion and black pepper to taste. Set aside.

Place the flour in a medium-sized bowl. Stuff the mushroom caps with the chorizo and beef mixture, making sure that the mixture is level with the edges of the mushroom and makes a dome shape at the centre. Lightly dust the entire mushroom and stuffing with flour, shaking off the excess.

Whisk together the two eggs in a small bowl and add a pinch of salt. Dredge each patty in the egg, dipping one mushroom at a time, coating all sides using a fork. Place on a rack to allow the excess egg to drip off.

Heat a large non-stick frying pan over a medium–low heat and drizzle in a generous amount of vegetable oil. Place the mushrooms, meat side down, in the pan and cook for about 3–4 minutes. Flip over and cook until the meat is done. Place on oil-absorbing paper and serve immediately with a wedge of lemon.

# Kimchi, Prosciutto, Pork and Chive Jeon
## Wanja Jeon

*These little meat patties are so easy to make, and are often served at room temperature, so they are perfect for lunches or for a quick snack. My mom used to make these and pack them for us to eat in the car during long rides. In this recipe, I have added prosciutto to boost the pork flavour and make these flat meatballs extra tasty.*

**Makes 8 small pancakes**

175g (6oz) pork mince
45g (1¾oz) prosciutto, finely chopped
100g (3½oz) tofu, drained and pressed to remove excess water (page 123)
35g (1¼oz) cabbage kimchi, finely chopped
¼ tsp garlic, grated or finely chopped
¼ tsp ginger, peeled and grated
2 shallots, finely chopped
4 tbsp chives, finely chopped, plus extra to serve
1 tsp roasted sesame oil
1 tsp roasted sesame seeds
1 tsp gochugaru (Korean chilli flakes)
2 tsp mirin
2 eggs
a pinch of salt
120g (3¾oz) rice flour
vegetable oil, for frying
Pancake Dipping Sauce (page 14), to serve

In a large bowl, mix together the pork, prosciutto, tofu (it will crumble as you mix), kimchi, garlic, ginger, shallots, chives, pepper, sesame oil, sesame seeds, gochugaru and mirin. Season to taste.

Crack the two eggs into a bowl, add the pinch of salt and beat well. Set aside. Put the rice flour in another bowl and set aside.

Using your hands, shape the meat mixture into small patties, about 50g (2oz) each. Dredge each patty in the rice flour, shaking off the excess, and place on a tray.

Heat a non-stick frying pan over a medium–low heat and drizzle with oil. Dip each patty into the egg mixture, then place carefully into the pan. Fry for about 4–5 minutes until cooked through, flipping once.

Serve immediately with the dipping sauce and sprinkle with fresh chives to garnish.

# Deep-fried Seaweed Spring Rolls

## Gimmari

*These delicately fried rolls are so light and crispy and full of flavour. A variation on the much-loved kimbap rolls, these logs are stuffed with sweet potato noodles instead of rice and offer a surprisingly fun, springy, toothsome texture.*

**Makes 8 spring rolls**

3 eggs
450g (1lb) japchae noodles (sweet potato noodles), cooked according to packet instructions
2 tbsp white sugar
2 tbsp roasted sesame oil
2 tbsp roasted sesame seeds, crushed
4 tsp soy sauce
½ tsp black pepper, freshly ground
1½ tsp salt
½ yellow pepper, julienned
½ red pepper, julienned
1 carrot, peeled and julienned
50g (2oz) long French beans, trimmed and julienned
100g (3½oz) purple kale, stems removed and julienned
8 large seaweed sheets, cut into 20 x 10cm (8 x 4in) sheets
potato flour, for dusting
sea salt
Pancake Dipping Sauce (page 14), to serve

BATTER
40g (1½oz) plain flour
100g (3½oz) potato flour
20g (¾oz) rice flour
150ml (5fl oz) tbsp vodka
120ml (4fl oz) soda water, chilled
vegetable oil, for frying

First, make an omelette by whisking the eggs together with a pinch of salt. Place a non-stick frying pan over a medium–low heat and drizzle with oil. Tip in the eggs, and allow to cook slowly, without stirring, to keep it flat. Cook until set, flipping once during cooking.

Place the noodles in a bowl, toss with the sugar, sesame oil, sesame seeds, soy sauce, black pepper and the 1½ tsp salt. Set aside.

Place a large saucepan of salted water over a high heat. Bring to the boil, and prepare an ice bath in a bowl. Blanch the yellow peppers first, immersing them in the boiling water for about 2–3 minutes until just softened. Remove with a slotted spoon and place in the ice bath, then in a colander to drain. Pat dry with kichen paper and sprinkle lightly with salt. Repeat for the red peppers, carrot, beans and kale.

Place a piece of seaweed on a flat surface, shiny side facing down. Lay a row of noodles (about 65g/2½oz) along the bottom edge, then add a row of red pepper, yellow pepper, beans, carrot and kale, taking care to pay attention to what colours are next to each other. Roll and seal by wetting the edge of the seaweed slightly and press firmly to close.

Half fill a heavy-based saucepan with oil and heat to 180°C (350°F) While the oil is heating, coat each gimmari with the potato flour, gently tapping off any access.

In a medium bowl, make the batter by whisking together the flours, vodka and soda. Working in batches, gently and quickly dip the gimmari into the batter and then place into the oil. Fry for about 5 minutes until crispy. Place on a cooling rack to to drain. Let the oil return to 180°C (350°F) before cooking the next batch. Keep previous batches warm in a low oven.

Serve immediately slicing in half, if you like, with a serrated knife, and serve with the pancake dipping sauce.

# Chicken Meatballs

*These little skewered chicken meatballs are the perfect pre-game starter. I love their gingery kick, and the thin flour coating helps them brown better, giving them a nice flavourful caramelized crusty outside. This recipe works well for making chicken burgers too, with Gochujang Mayonnaise slathered on top.*

**Makes 20 meatballs**

500g (1lb 2oz) chicken mince, preferably thigh meat
3 spring onions, thinly sliced at an angle
2 tsp garlic, peeled and grated
1 tbsp ginger, peeled and grated
1 egg, beaten
50g (2oz) panko breadcrumbs
2 tsp whole milk
2 tbsp gochujang (Korean chilli paste)
1 tsp soy sauce
2 tsp brown sugar
1½ tsp sea salt
½ tsp black pepper
3 tbsp plain flour
vegetable oil, for frying

TO SERVE
a pinch of roasted black sesame seeds
3 tbsp Sriracha or Gochujang Mayonnaise
  (page 14), for dipping

For the meatballs, in a large bowl, gently mix together the chicken mince, spring onions, garlic, ginger, egg, panko, milk, gochujang, soy sauce, brown sugar, salt and pepper. Form the mixture into about 20 golf ball-sized (35g/1¼oz) meatballs.

Spoon the flour onto a plate, then roll the meatballs in the flour, shaking off the excess.

Heat a non-stick frying pan over a medium–high heat. Drizzle generously with oil. Working in batches so as not to overcrowd the pan, place the meatballs in the pan and fry for about 5–6 minutes, until cooked through, rotating often to cook evenly.

Serve the meatballs immediately with skewers, garnished with chives and sesame seeds, with Sriracha or gochujang mayonnaise on the side.

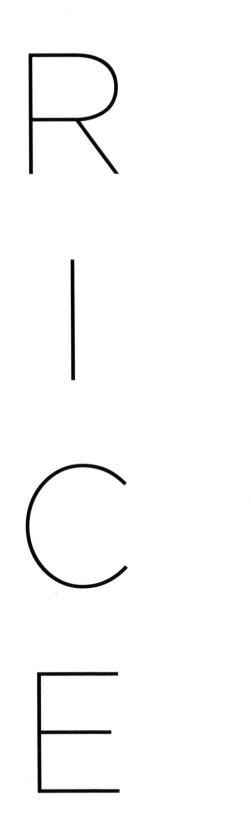

When people ask you if you have eaten
in Korea, they literally ask you if you have
had rice. And often people do not feel as
if they are full without these pearly polished
grains as part of their meal. These days, brown,
black and multigrain rice are en vogue, and a
good thing, as they are much healthier for you.
Rice cakes, tteok, are chewy logs or discs
made of rice flour. Their addictive toothsome
texture makes them a well-loved ingredient
in so many dishes.

# English Bibim-Breakfast

*When we launched our brunch menu at my restaurant, we wanted to offer some traditional fare, so the Bibim Breakfast came to fruition. The Tonkatsu Gochujang Ketchup sauce is reminiscent of English HP sauce, with a spicy kick and tastes delish with breakfast meats. I love the surprise potato 'gamja jeon' on the bottom, which is a nod to a traditional rosti or latka.*

**Serves 2**

2 good-quality sausages
6 streaky bacon slices
2 bunches baby cherry tomatoes on the vine
3 tbsp extra virgin olive oil
1 spring of thyme
1 spring of oregano
300g (11oz) shimeji mushrooms, bottoms trimmed
½ tsp garlic, grated
120g (3¾oz) baby spinach
2 duck eggs
2 tbsp white wine vinegar
2 slices sourdough
sea salt and freshly ground black pepper

TONKATSU GOCHUJANG KETCHUP
1 tbsp gochujang (Korean chilli paste)
3½ tbsp tomato ketchup
3½ tbsp tonkatsu sauce

PURPLE POTATO ROSTI (GAMJA JEON)
1 large purple potato, peeled
¼ onion, peeled
½ egg, beaten
1 tbsp plain flour
½ tsp coarse kosher salt (or ¼ tsp fine sea salt), plus extra to sprinkle
¼ tsp baking powder
a pinch of freshly ground black pepper
vegetable oil, for frying

First, make the sauce. In a small bowl, whisk together all the ingredients until well incorporated. Cover and store in the fridge until needed.

To make the rosti, grate the potato and onion on a box grater or food processor with a coarse grating disk. Transfer the mixture to a clean tea towel and wring out as much liquid as possible. Working quickly, transfer the mixture to a large bowl. Add the egg, flour, salt, baking powder and pepper and mix until the flour is absorbed.

In a medium heavy-based pan set over a medium-high heat, pour in about 5mm (¼in) of vegetable oil. Once the oil is hot (a drop of batter placed in the pan should sizzle), divide the batter into half and spoon one half into the pan. Use a spatula to flatten and shape it into a disc about 2cm (¾in) thick and 10cm (4in) in diameter. Fry until the edges of the rosti are brown and crispy, about 5 minutes, then flip and cook until the other side is deep brown, about another 5 minutes. Remove from the pan and drain on kitchen paper. Sprinkle with salt and then keep warm while you repeat the process and cook the other half of the batter.

Preheat the oven to 180°C fan/200°C/400°F/gas 6. Place the sausages on a baking sheet and cook for 20–25 minutes, until thoroughly cooked, turning halfway through the cooking time, or according to specific packet instructions. Sausages should be cooked until the juices run clear when pierced with a fork and there is no pink meat. Keep warm, leaving the oven on to cook the bacon.

Lay the streaky bacon on a baking sheet lined with parchment, place another piece of paper on top of the bacon and place another tray on top. This will keep the bacon flat. Place in the oven and cook for 10–12 minutes, until golden and crispy. Keep warm.

For the roasted cherry tomatoes, place the vines into a small roasting tin, drizzle with the extra virgin olive oil, toss in the thyme and oregano and season with salt and pepper. Roast in the oven for 10 minutes, until the tomatoes are just tender. Remove from the heat and keep warm.

To cook the mushrooms, heat a drizzle of oil in a large heavy-based frying pan over a medium heat. Add the mushrooms, garlic and salt and black pepper to taste. Sauté for 5 minutes, stirring, until the mushrooms are lightly browned. Remove from the pan and set aside in a warm place.

Add a touch more oil to the same pan then toss in the spinach and cook for about 3–5 minutes until wilted. Season with salt and pepper to taste. Remove from the heat and keep warm.

For the duck eggs, bring a large pan of water to the boil and add the white wine vinegar. Crack the eggs into two individual cups. Using a whisk, stir the vinegar water vigorously to create a whirlpool. Working quickly, gently place the eggs one by one into the centre of the whirlpool and allow the water to return to a simmer. Poach for about 3 minutes until still runny inside. Lift from the water with a slotted spoon and keep warm.

Heat a griddle pan over a high heat and place the slices of sourdough bread in the pan. Cook until toasted and griddle marks appear on the bread, then cut each slice in half. Set aside.

Place a dolsot bowl over a medium–high heat and place the potato pancake on the bottom. Arrange half the sausage, bacon, tomatoes, mushrooms, spinach and a duck egg on top. Tuck the slices of bread in as well on the side. Repeat to fill a second bowl.

Serve immediately with the tonkatsu sauce on the side and a sprinkle of sesame seeds to finish.

# Vegan Bowl with Cauliflower Rice

*Plant-based dishes are so popular right now, and I find that Korean food is easily adaptable to this diet due to its deep tradition of Buddhism. I am also a massive lover of vegetables, so developing this nutritious bowl was a delight.*

**Serves 2**

300g (11oz) cauliflower, stems removed and cut into florets
3 tbsp Vegetarian Dashi Stock (page 22) or water
50g (2oz) purple kale, stems removed and shredded
50g (2oz) green kale, stems removed and shredded
2 tsp lime juice
8 baby carrots, peeled and trimmed
400g (14oz) raw tofu, drained, pressed and cut into 2cm (¾in) dice (page 123)
90g (3oz) edamame beans, pods and skins removed
½ beetroot, peeled, thinly sliced on a mandoline, and julienned
5 chives, cut into 1cm (½in) pieces
2 tsp kazami nori (shredded seaweed)
sea salt

DRESSING
4 tsp white miso
5 tsp mirin
½ tsp roasted sesame oil

TO SERVE
mixed nuts
black and white sesame seeds
pumpkin seeds
mixed seeds
goji berries

For the dressing, whisk all the ingredients together well. Set aside.

Place the cauliflower florets in a food processor and pulse several times until the cauliflower looks like a coarse meal.

In a large non-stick frying pan set over a medium heat, tip in the cauliflower and the vegetarian dashi stock or water and sauté for about 9–10 minutes until softened and dried out. Remove from the heat and set aside.

In a large bowl, both kinds of kale with the lime juice. Massage the kale with your hands well for about 1 minute and set aside to soften for 3–4 minutes to break down the chewy fibres.

Fill a large saucepan with salted water and bring to the boil; meanwhile, prepare an ice bath in a bowl on the side. Blanch the carrots by plunging them in the boiling water for about 3–4 minutes until softened. Take the carrots out using a slotted spoon and immediately immerse them in the ice bath. Remove and cut in half lengthways, then season with salt.

Heat a non-stick sauté pan over a medium heat and toast the nuts and seeds until golden brown. Remove from the heat and set aside.

Divide the cauliflower evenly between two large bowls and arrange the tofu, kale, carrots, edamame and beetroot on the top. Top with the chives and kazami nori, then sprinkle the nuts, sesame seeds, mixed seeds and goji berries on top. Drizzle the dressing over the top. Serve warm or at room temperature.

# Rice Cake Skewers

## Tteok Kochi

*On the streets of Seoul, you'll find so many treats on sticks, and rice cakes are in abundance. Served both sweet and savoury, these toothsome chewy and totally addictive skewers are a fantastic appetizer or snack. My father's favourite one is the simple, yet perfectly balanced, savoury version with just roasted sesame oil brushed on top and sprinkled with sea salt. I love it too!*

SAVOURY VERSIONS

1  Wrap the rice cakes with with kimchi and bacon before grilling them

2  Brush with Sweet Soy Sauce (page 77)

3  Brush with roasted sesame oil and sprinkle with roasted, chopped hazelnuts

4  Brush with Gochujang Sauce (page 14) and sprinkle with black sesame seeds

SWEET VERSIONS

Using a pastry brush, brush the rice cakes with honey, and sprinkle with any of the following:

5  desiccated coconut

6  daechu (dried jujube dates)

7  toasted mixed seeds and dried fruit

8  toasted chopped mixed nuts (such as pecans and peanuts)

9  roasted black and white sesame seeds

10  misugaru (Korean roasted grain powder)

Blanch the rice cakes in boiling water for about 30 seconds to soften them. Drain, then run them under cold water. Drain again and pat dry.

Skewer the rice cakes with bamboo sticks and chargrill them on a lightly oiled griddle pan set over a medium–high heat. Grill both sides of the rice cakes for 2–3 minutes on each side.

Remove from the heat and brush your sauce of choice on both sides of the rice cakes. Sprinkle with your choice of topping.

# Kimchi Lamb Biryani

*I developed this dish when I was asked to collaborate with a local Indian Biryani restaurant. We all loved it so much, particularly the raita, that I had to include it in this book. The lamb stir-fry is so incredibly tasty on its own as well. I guarantee that this is the best KorIndian dish you've tasted!*

**Makes 2 large bowls**

120g (3¾oz) gochujang (Korean chilli paste)
5 garlic cloves, grated
1 tbsp ginger, peeled and grated
1½ tbsp mirin
1½ tbsp soy sauce
1½ tbsp roasted sesame oil
1 tsp white sugar
1½ tbsp pear or apple juice
½ tsp freshly ground black pepper
500g (1lb 2oz) leg of lamb, trimmed and cut into 3cm (1¼in) cubes
3 spring onions, finely sliced

PERILLA LEAF AND YUJA RAITA
200g (7oz) Greek yoghurt
50g (2oz) Cucumber and Yuja Pickle (page 49), cut into 5mm (¼in) dice
4 perilla leaves, shredded
1 shallot, finely diced
a large pinch of caster sugar
sprinkle of ground cumin (optional)
sea salt

KIMCHI FRIED RICE
250g (9oz) basmati rice
80g (3oz) onion, finely diced
80g (3oz) carrot, peeled and finely diced
80g (3oz) mushrooms, finely diced
80g (3oz) courgette, finely diced
350g (12oz) cabbage kimchi, finely diced
4 perilla leaves, chopped into 1cm (½in) pieces
vegetable oil, for frying
sea salt

TO ASSEMBLE
1 egg, beaten
240g (9oz) Hotteok dough (page 191; make a quarter recipe of the dough)
plain flour, for rolling

For the lamb stir-fry, in a medium bowl, whisk together the gochujang, garlic, ginger, mirin, soy sauce, sesame oil, sugar, pear juice, black pepper and 4 tablespoons water, until well incorporated. Place the lamb into a large food-safe plastic bag and tip in the marinade. Seal the bag and massage the marinade into the meat until well coated. Marinate the lamb for up to 24 hours in advance for best results.

To make the raita, in a small bowl, mix together the yoghurt, cucumber pickle, perilla leaves, shallots and sugar and season with salt to taste. Sprinkle cumin on top before serving, if desired. Set aside.

For the kimchi fried rice, cook the basmati rice according to the packet instructions and leave to one side. In a non-stick pan set over a medium–high heat, drizzle in a little vegetable oil and tip in the onion, carrot, mushrooms and courgette. Cook for 2–3 minutes, until softened, then add the rice and cook for a further 2 minutes, tossing until well incorporated. Add the chopped kimchi and perilla leaves and cook for a further 2–3 minutes, mixing it well into the rice. Season with sea salt, to taste. Cover and keep warm while you cook the lamb.

Place a non-stick frying pan over a medium–high heat. Tip in the lamb and all of the marinade. Sauté the lamb for about 5–6 minutes until it is cooked to medium·rare, and slightly caramelized on the edges. Toss in the spring onions. Add a touch of water if any liquid looks oily, stir until it becomes creamy and remove from the heat.

To assemble the dish, preheat the oven to 180°C fan/200°C/400°F/gas 6. Into two dolsot stone bowls, put a few scoops of rice, then some lamb, and then more rice and top with lamb. In a small bowl, whisk together the egg and a splash of water to make an egg wash. Brush the rim of the bowls with the egg wash. Divide the hotteok dough in half and roll out each piece on a floured surface to a circle slightly bigger than the bowls. Cover the top of the bowls entirely and seal around edges. Brush the tops with egg wash and make a hole in the centre of each with a knife. Bake for 10 minutes until golden brown. Serve with raita on the side.

# Bibimbap with Prawns and Seasonal Vegetables

*Bibimbap has quickly become one of Korea's most popular exports. It really is a perfect meal in a single bowl – teaming with gorgeous bright veggies and your choice of protein, pleasing vegetarians and meat-lovers alike. I like to add a mix of veggies that are raw and fresh, or have been sautéed or pickled to add variation in texture and flavour.*

**Serves 2**

6 rainbow baby carrots, peeled and trimmed
6 tenderstem broccoli, trimmed
½ bunch purple kalettes, trimmed
6 prawns, cleaned, deshelled and deveined
2 tbsp roasted sesame oil
400g (14oz) steamed white rice
60g (2½oz) Seasoned Spinach (page 26)
60g (2½oz) Stir-fried hobak (Korean Courgette) (page 29)
60g (2½oz) Spicy Pickled Radish Salad (page 22)
handful of ssukgat (chrysanthemum leaves)
2 tbsp red tobiko (flying fish roe)
2 fried eggs
sea salt and freshly ground black pepper
½ quantity of Gochujang Sauce (page 14), to serve

FRIED CHICKPEAS WITH GOCHUGARU
60g (2½oz) canned chickpeas in water, rinsed and drained
¼ tsp gochugaru (Korean chilli flakes)
vegetable oil, for frying
sea salt

First, make the deep-fried chickpeas. Pour oil to a depth of 5cm (2in) into a heavy–based pan, place over a medium heat, and warm until it reaches 160°C (320°F) on a frying thermometer. Add the chickpeas to the oil and cook for 2–3 minutes; their colour should slightly darken and the outside become crunchy. Remove using a slotted spoon and drain thoroughly on kitchen paper, then toss with the gochugaru and salt while still hot. Set aside.

Bring a large saucepan of salted water to the boil and prepare an ice bath in a bowl on the side. Blanch the carrots for 3–4 minutes until tender, then remove from the hot water with a slotted spoon and plunge into the ice bath to stop cooking. Remove and season with salt. Do the same with the tenderstem broccoli and the kalettes. Set aside.

For the prawns, heat a drizzle of oil in a frying pan, add the prawns and cook for 1–2 minutes on each side until cooked through. Remove from the heat, and season with salt and pepper to taste.

To assemble the bibimbab, set two dolsot stone pots over a medium heat. Add 1 tablespoon of the sesame oil to each pot and coat the base of the pot. Divide the rice between the bowls, spreading it evenly to cover the bottom of the bowl. Cook, undisturbed, for 6–8 minutes until you can hear sizzling from the bottom, and the rice develops a golden crust.

Divide all of the vegetables and chickpeas between the bowls and arrange in sections on top of the rice. Finally, arrange the prawns on the rice, as you like. Top with chrysanthemum leaves, tobiko and a fried egg.

Serve immediately with the gochujang sauce on the side.

# Pimped Out Tteokbokki

*I have so many memories of eating tteokbokki on the side of the street at 3am with toothpicks in Seoul. It is still one of my favourite late-night meals to help soak up all of the alcohol! These days, there are so many versions with so many ingredients that it seems a bit like a culinary landfill. Make this dish for a group and cook it at the table if you can – your guests will have so much fun.*

**Serves 4–6**

450g (1lb) rice cakes, of all different
  shapes and kinds, soaked in cold water
  for 15–30 minutes, then drained
1 pack instant ramyun (ramen) noodles
80g (3oz) jjolmyeon (chewy noodles),
  cooked according to packet instructions
160g (5¾oz) eomuk (fish cake sheets)
3 fried dumplings (shop-bought are fine)
5 pieces yubu (fried tofu)
1 small red onion, thinly sliced
1 large carrot, peeled and cut into 1 x 4cm
  (½ x 1½in) pieces
4 spring onions, cut into 4cm (1½in) pieces
  at an angle
1 egg, soft boiled and cut into quarters
30g (1oz) garlic chives
¼ head Chinese cabbage, cut into
  4cm (1½in) pieces
10 cooked cocktail sausages
100g (3½oz) Spam, cut into matchsticks
1 red chilli, thinly sliced at an angle

TTEOKBOKKI SAUCE
15 myulchi (large dried anchovies),
  heads and guts removed
10cm (4in) piece of dashima (dried kelp)
2 garlic cloves, grated or finely chopped
35g (1¼oz) gochujang (Korean chilli paste)
2 tbsp white sugar
1 tbsp gochugaru (Korean chilli flakes)
1 tbsp soy sauce
100g (3½oz) danmuji (yellow pickled radish),
  thinly sliced on a mandoline, to serve

In a medium saucepan, make the sauce by combining the myulchi, dashima and 1.2 litres (2 pints) water and bring to the boil. Reduce the heat to a simmer and cook for about 20 minutes. Pass the anchovy stock through a fine-mesh sieve into another pan, then discard the solids.

In a separate pan, pour in about 500ml (17fl oz) of the stock (reserving the rest) and bring to a simmer. Add the garlic, gochujang, sugar, gochugaru and soy sauce, whisking well until everything is dissolved.

In a large, wide, deep pan, arrange the rice cakes, both kinds of noodles, fish cakes, dumplings, yubu, red onion, carrots, spring onion, egg, garlic chives, cabbage, sausages, Spam and chilli. Pour in the sauce, cover with a lid and bring to a simmer over a medium–high heat. Uncover and cook for a further 2–3 minutes, mixing, until the noodles are cooked, adding more stock if necessary as the broth boils down. Serve immediately with danmuji on the side.

# Tteok with Perilla Leaf Pesto

*Perilla leaves, often mistakenly called sesame leaves, harbour a distinctive herby flavour that is a cross between basil and mint, with grassy notes and a subtle anise fragrance. As a result, perilla works so well in pesto. I have put this pesto recipe on the menu at my restaurant in many forms – with burrata and heirloom tomatoes, and with tteok 'pasta'. It is always a hit, and the look of surprise and delight on diners' faces is always rewarding.*

**Serves 4**

400g (14oz) garaetteok (long, thick rice
  cakes), dried until hard
40g (1½ oz) salt
2 tsp roasted pine nuts
2 perilla leaves, shredded
sea salt and freshly ground black pepper

PERILLA LEAF PESTO
½ tbsp garlic, chopped
45g (1½oz) perilla leaves, stems trimmed,
  and leaves roughly chopped
30g (1oz) pine nuts, very lightly toasted
4 tsp roasted sesame seeds
1½ tbsp roasted sesame oil
65ml (2¼fl oz) yuja (yuzu) juice
1 tsp honey
80ml (2½fl oz) extra virgin olive oil

To make the pesto, place the garlic, perilla leaves, pine nuts, sesame seeds, sesame oil, yuja juice and honey together in a food processor, and pulse until puréed. Slowly add the olive oil, season generously with salt and pepper, and set aside.

Shave the garaetteok using a mandoline to make long flat rice cake 'sheets', about 2–3mm (⅛in) thickness. Cut them lengthways into long, thin 'noodles', about 3mm (⅛in) wide.

In a large saucepan, boil about 4 litres (7 pints) water with 40g (1½oz) salt. Once boiling, add the rice cake noodles and stir to prevent them sticking together. Cook for 30 seconds, or until the noodles are soft, then drain the noodles and transfer them to a large bowl.

Immediately mix the pesto into the rice cake noodles. Stir in the toasted pine nuts and perilla leaves and season with salt and pepper. Serve immediately.

# Tteok Carbonara

*Rome is one of my most loved cities, and I have so many memories of gorging on spaghetti carbonara. I love the rich creaminess from the eggs and cheese, so I decided to try it with rice cakes. It is an interesting twist and way to eat tteok, and works well as a surprisingly tasty appetizer.*

**Serves 4**

400g (14oz) garaetteok (long, thick rice cakes), dried out until hard
40g (1½oz) salt
vegetable oil, for frying
1–2 tbsp extra virgin olive oil, plus extra to drizzle
50g (2oz) pancetta, diced
4 egg yolks
15g (½oz) pecorino, grated
sea salt and freshly ground black pepper

Shave the garaetteok through a mandoline to make long, flat rice cake sheets, about 2–3mm (⅛in) thickness.

In a large saucepan, boil 4 litres (7 pints) water with 40g (1½oz) salt.

In the meantime, drizzle a little oil into a large frying pan and fry the pancetta over a medium–high heat for about 5 minutes until golden and crispy.

In a small bowl, whisk together the egg yolks and cheese, and set aside.

Once the water is boiling, add the rice cake pasta and stir to prevent it sticking together. Cook for 30 seconds, or until the pasta is soft, then drain, transfer to a large bowl and quickly toss with the 1–2 tablespoons of olive oil to coat. Reserve 120ml (4fl oz) of cooking water.

Add the rice pasta to the frying pan with the pancetta, set over a low heat, and add the egg and cheese mixture. Mix together, adding some of the cooking water to achieve a creamy consistency.

Season with salt and freshly ground pepper to taste, and serve immediately.

# Bibimbap with Wild Mushrooms and Raw Beef

*I am a big fan of steak tartare, and Korea's version, yook hwe, doesn't disappoint. In my version below, I use white miso to add depth and a soul-satisfying flavour to the beef. The wild mushrooms bring an earthy nuttiness to the bowl as well, with a little hint of golden butter to make it all silky delicious.*

**Serves 2 as a starter**

2 tsp roasted sesame oil
200g (7oz) cooked rice

MUSHROOMS
40g (1½oz) butter
400g (14oz) mixed wild mushrooms,
   trimmed, stems removed and cut into
   5mm (¼in) slices
2 tsp chives, chopped
1 tsp roasted sesame oil
sea salt and freshly ground black pepper

BEEF
220g (8oz) beef fillet steak (preferably
   prime), trimmed and diced
2 tsp shallot, chopped
1 tsp roasted sesame oil
1 tbsp soy sauce
2 tsp mirin
1½ tbsp white miso

TO SERVE
2 quail egg yolks
Lotus Crisps (page 21)
gim (roasted seaweed)

First, set two dolsot stone pots over a medium heat. Add 1 teaspoon of the sesame oil to each bowl and coat the base of the bowl.

Divide the cooked rice between the bowls. Spread the rice evenly over the bottom and cook, undisturbed, for 4–5 minutes until the bottom of the rice develops a golden crust. This should be about the same time the toppings are done, but if the rice is ready beforehand, just turn off the heat.

For the mushrooms, place a non-stick frying pan over a medium–high heat. Add the butter and toss in the mushrooms. Sauté until wilted and cooked through, about 4–5 minutes. Toss in the chives and drizzle in the sesame oil. Toss to coat, remove from the heat and arrange the mushrooms on the rice.

In a medium bowl, toss together the beef, shallot, sesame oil, soy sauce, mirin, white miso and salt and pepper to taste. Arrange the beef on the rice.

Make a small well in each mound of beef and put an egg yolk in each. Top with lotus crips. Serve immediately with gim, on the side.

# Royal Tteokbokki

*Although the spicy version of tteokbokki is better known, the original dish, which hails from the royal court of the Chosun dynasty, has no chillies at all. Instead, it boasts a lip-smacking, salty-sweet sauce with black pepper undertones. It is also super quick to make – a crowd-pleasing stir-fry that even the kids will love.*

## Serves 4

450g (1lb) beef rib eye, trimmed and thinly sliced (about 5mm/¼in thick)
1 small firm but ripe pear, grated
3 tbsp brown sugar
3 tbsp soy sauce
2 tbsp roasted sesame oil
1 tbsp vegetable oil, plus a drizzle for the stir-fry
5 garlic cloves, grated
2 tbsp roasted sesame seeds, crushed
¼ tsp ginger, peeled and grated
½ tsp black pepper

STIR-FRY
280g (10oz) tteok (thin rice cake batons)
50g (2oz) baby onions, peeled and quartered
120g (3¾oz) mixed wild mushrooms (I like to use 2 large oyster mushrooms, sliced, with ½ bunch enoki mushrooms)
1 rainbow carrot, peeled and julienned
100g (3½oz) baby leeks, trimmed and cut lengthways into quarters
80g (3oz) baby corn, cut lengthways into quarters

TO SERVE
1 spring onion
1 quail egg, soft boiled
a pinch of black sesame seeds

In a shallow dish, combine the beef, pear and brown sugar and massage with your hands to thoroughly combine. Leave to marinate for about 30 minutes at room temperature. Meanwhile, in a large bowl, stir together the soy sauce, sesame oil, vegetable oil, garlic, crushed sesame seeds, ginger and black pepper. Set aside.

When the beef is ready, use your hands to shake off and squeeze out any excess sugary liquid, then add the beef to the soy sauce marinade. Toss to coat, cover and marinate for about 30 minutes at room temperature, or overnight in the fridge.

Meanwhile, cut the spring onion lengthways into thin strips and soak in iced water until curled, then drain.

About 30 minutes before cooking, place the tteok in a large bowl with enough water to cover them. Leave them to rehydrate.

Once the tteok are rehydrated, remove from the water, retaining 4 tablespoons of liquid. Heat a drizzle of vegetable oil in a large frying pan over a medium heat. Add the baby onions and cook for 6–8 minutes until softened. Add the mushrooms, carrot, baby leeks and baby corn and cook for a further 5 minutes until slightly softened.

Increase the heat to medium–high, add the beef, marinade rehydrated tteok and the retained water. Cook for 2–3 minutes, stirring occasionally, until the meat is medium rare, and slightly pink in the centre. Transfer to a serving plate, and arrange the spring onion and quail egg on top. Finish with a sprinkle of black sesame seeds.

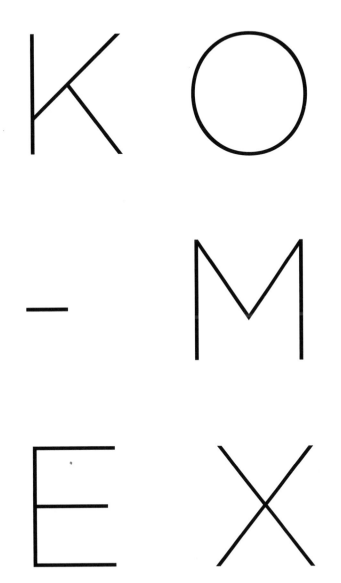

The popularity of Korean–Mexican cuisine has quickly spread across the USA. I had my first Korean taco in San Antonio, Texas and it was a revelation. Korean spices marry beautifully with Mexican flavours, making this pairing a winner.

# Sea Bass Tacos

*I love tempura and tacos, so this recipe is pretty much a showstopper for me. Light, crispy fried sea bass, topped with a refreshing spicy kimchi salsa and crispy bright slaw makes such a tasty combination. These are the perfect light lunch.*

**Makes 8 tacos**

120g (3¾oz) tempura flour
110ml (3¾fl oz) soda water
200g (7oz) sea bass fillets, skin
   removed, deboned and cut into
   2 x 4cm (¾ x 1½in) strips
vegetable oil, for frying
sea salt

KIMCHI SALSA
100g (3½oz) cabbage kimchi, chopped
   into 5mm (¼in) pieces
20g (¾oz) tomato, diced into 5mm (¼in)
   pieces
20g (¾oz) pickled jalapeños, diced into
   5mm (¼in) pieces

SLAW
4 tsp yuja (yuzu) juice
3 tbsp Kewpie mayonnaise
½ red onion, thinly sliced
½ cucumber, deseeded and julienned
½ Asian pear, peeled and julienned

TO SERVE
8 taco shells, 12cm (5in) diameter
8 tsp soured cream
1 small tomato, finely diced
baby coriander

First, make the kimchi salsa. In a medium bowl, toss together the kimchi, tomato and jalapeños until evenly mixed, then set aside.

Next, to make the slaw, whisk the yuja juice and mayonnaise together in a medium bowl. Stir in the red onion, cucumber and pear. Cover and leave in the fridge.

Half fill a heavy-based saucepan with oil and heat to 180°C (350°F).

Make the tempura batter just before frying. In a bowl, whisk together the tempura flour and soda water, making sure to keep it lumpy.

Salt the sea bass on both sides. Working in batches, dip the fish into the tempura batter, and fry for about 3–4 minutes until the batter is golden brown and the fish is cooked. Place on a rack to drain off any excess oil and keep warm while you cook the rest.

Heat up the taco shells according to the packet instructions.

Line the shells up on a plate and add a piece of fish to each one. Top with the slaw and then the salsa. Garnish with a dollop of soured cream, diced tomato and baby coriander.

# Korean Chicken Quesadilla

*Quesadillas are so popular, and the combination of kimchi and cheese here makes this version extra tasty. I like to stuff my quesadillas full of goodness: sweet caramelized soy chicken, tangy kimchi, spicy jalapeños, and gooey creamy sharp Cheddar cheese. Make these for match day and your family will love you!*

**Serves 4**

550g (1lb 4oz) chicken thighs,
    diced into 3cm (1¼in) pieces
vegetable oil, for cooking
100g (3½oz) cabbage kimchi,
    grilled and chopped
20g (¾oz) pickled jalapeños,
    finely chopped
250g (9oz) extra mature Cheddar cheese,
    grated
1 tsp finely chopped coriander
4 flour tortillas, 25cm (10in) diameter
sea salt

MARINADE
3 tbsp soy sauce
2½ tbsp mirin
2 tsp white sugar
2 tsp garlic, grated or finely chopped
1½ tsp ginger, peeled and grated

TO SERVE
4 tbsp soured cream
2 spring onions, cut lengthways into thin
    strips, soaked in iced water until curled,
    then drained
½ red chilli, thinly sliced
½ green chilli, thinly siced

First make the marinade. In a medium bowl, stir together the soy sauce, mirin, sugar, garlic and ginger. Add the chicken and marinate at room temperature for about 30 minutes, or cover and refrigerate up to overnight.

Heat a large frying pan over a medium–high heat with a drizzle of vegetable oil. Add the chicken and cook for 5 minutes, stirring occasionally, until the meat is cooked through and golden and lightly charred in spots. Remove from the heat and set aside.

In a medium bowl, place the chicken, kimchi, jalapeños, cheese and coriander and mix thoroughly, breaking up the chicken.

Spread half of the mixed ingredients evenly over one of the tortillas, leaving a 1cm (½in) border. Place another tortilla on top, then press down. Repeat for the second set of tortillas with the remaining filling.

In a 25cm (10in) non-stick frying pan, heat tablespoon of oil over a medium heat. Place one of the assembled tortillas in the pan and cook for about 2 minutes. Gently move the tortilla around until golden brown and puffy on one side. Flip the quesadilla with a flexible spatula, to cook the other side for another 2 minutes. Season with salt, and cook until golden brown and the cheese is melted inside. Repeat with other quesadilla.

Leave the quesadillas on a kitchen paper to drain. Cut into wedges and serve while still warm, sprinkled with soured cream, spring onions and chillies.

# Kimchi Lamb Tamales

*My friend Vivian and I once did a tour of the tamale ladies of New York, driving around Spanish Harlem at some obscenely early hour on a Sunday to buy fresh handmade tamales. These cute Mexican grandmothers simply hang out on random street corners, selling them from coolers or little shopping trollies. Since then, I have had a strong love for these fluffy tied-up treasures.*

**Makes 35–40 tamales**

3 whole dried ancho chillies,
  deseeded and stems removed
3 whole dried guajillo chillies,
  deseeded and stems removed
100g (3½oz) chipotle paste
10 garlic cloves, smashed
juice of 4 mandarins
  (about 190ml/6½fl oz)
2 tbsp yuja (yuzu) juice
2 tbsp extra virgin olive oil
3 tbsp soy sauce
3 tbsp fish sauce
1 tbsp mirin
1 tbsp ground cumin
2 tbsp brown sugar
1.35kg (3lb) lamb shoulder, bone in
2 onions, roughly chopped
2 carrots, peeled and roughly chopped
350g (12oz) cabbage kimchi,
  finely chopped
sea salt and freshly ground black pepper

CORN FILLING
620g (1lb 6oz) masa harina (Mexican
  corn flour)
1.32 litres (2¼ pints) chicken stock
450g (1lb) lard, cut into 2cm (¾in) cubes,
  softened at room temperature
2 tsp sea salt
4 tsp baking powder

TO ASSEMBLE
45–50 dried corn husks, soaked in water
  for 1 hour
35–40 perilla leaves

Start with the lamb. Preheat the oven to 160°C fan/180°C/350°F/gas 4 and adjust the shelf to the lowest position.

Boil about 750ml (26fl oz) water and pour into a heatproof bowl. Soak the dried chillies for 3–4 minutes until softened, then strain, reserving the liquid.

Place the chillies into a blender and add the chipotle paste, garlic, mandarin juice, yuja juice, olive oil, soy sauce, fish sauce, mirin, cumin and brown sugar. Blend until smooth.

Score the fat on the lamb shoulder and season it well on all sides. Place the lamb shoulder in a large casserole dish, fat side up. Pour in the chilli mixture and, if necessary, add just enough of the reserved chilli water to have about 2.5cm (1in) of liquid on the bottom of the dish. Throw in the onions and carrots. Cover with a lid and cook for about 4–4½ hours until the lamb is tender and falls easily off the bone, basting the meat often during cooking.

Next make the corn filling for the tamales. In a large bowl, mix the masa harina with 1 litre (1¾ pints) of chicken stock. Cover with clingfilm and allow it to rest at room temperature for 15 minutes.

Place the lard in the bowl of a stand mixer. Using the paddle attachment, beat at high speed until uniform. Add the salt and baking powder and mix for about 2 minutes more until fully incorporated.

Pour the masa mixture into the lard a little at a time, allowing it to mix in well on a medium–high speed before adding the next bit. Once all the masa has been added, pour in enough of the remaining chicken stock, a little at a time, until the mixture is a light spreadable consistency; reserve the leftover stock. Cover the mixture with clingfilm and place in the fridge to chill for about 2 hours.

Before building the tamales, remove the masa from the fridge and beat again to make it spreadable, adding more chicken stock if necessary. Do a float test by filling a glass with cold water then dropping in a small ball of dough. It should float; if not, add a bit more chicken stock to the masa mixture and perform the test again, until the dough floats to the surface.

When the lamb is cooked, remove it from the dish, allow to cool slightly, then pull apart the meat. Skim the fat off the top of the sauce left in the dish, then return the pulled lamb back to the dish and mix with the sauce.

Add the kimchi to the dish containing the lamb, mix together and then set aside.

To assemble the tamales: on a flat surface, place a corn husk. Place a perilla leaf and 2-3 tablespoons of the masa dough on the wider side of the husk. Leaving a 2.5cm (1in) border around the edge, spread the dough into a rectangle 5mm (¼in) thick. Down the centre of the dough, place a tablespoon of the lamb filling in a line. Fold the bottom of the husk up, then fold over the sides. Tie the top with a thin strip of husk to secure. Repeat with the others.

In a large pan with a steamer insert, pour water to a depth of 2.5cm (1in) and bring to the boil. Place the tamales in the steamer basket, keeping them upright, and making sure the water is not higher than the bottom of the steamer basket. Cover and leave over a low heat for about 1 hour until the dough is cooked. Keep topping up the water as it evaporates. Once the corn filling pulls away easily from the husk, remove the tamales from the steamer. Leave them to cool for about 15 minutes until the dough firms up. Serve, or store in the refrigerator or freezer. To defrost and reheat the tamales, warm them in a steamer or in the microwave on high power for about 2 minutes.

# Korean Marinated Tofu Burritos

*Tofu is another one of my favourite foods. In Korea, it is a commonly used ingredient, and is often mixed with meat. This seasoning sauce turned out so well, Mi Kyung, my co-author, fell in love with this recipe. Feel free to try this marinade on fish, seafood and even chicken.*

**Makes 4 burritos**

400g (14oz) firm tofu
4 tbsp soy sauce
1 tbsp mirin
2 tbsp gochugaru (Korean chilli flakes)
1 tbsp roasted sesame oil
1 tsp garlic, grated or finely chopped
1 tsp ginger, peeled and grated
1 spring onion, thinly sliced at an angle
vegetable oil, for frying

BURRITO
4 large flour tortillas, 25cm (10in)
   diameter
400g (14oz) Kimchi Fried Rice
   (page 100)
160g (5¾oz) canned black beans,
   drained
½ avocado, peeled, pitted and sliced
   into 1cm (½in) thick pieces
½ beefsteak tomato, finely chopped
80g (3oz) baby spinach
4 tbsp soured cream

Place the tofu on a large plate with a few pieces of kitchen paper and place another plate on top. Leave to stand for 8–10 minutes to press and drain the water out. Cut the tofu into 2 x 2cm (¾ x ¾in) dice and place into a food-safe plastic bag.

In a small bowl, whisk together the soy sauce, mirin, gochugaru, sesame oil, garlic, ginger and spring onion. Tip the mixture into the bag with the tofu and allow to marinate in the fridge for about 30 minutes.

Place a non-stick frying pan over a medium–low heat and drizzle lightly with vegetable oil to coat the bottom of the pan. Pour in the tofu and marinating liquid and sauté for about 4–5 minutes, turning often, until warmed through and the tofu is slightly crispy. Remove from the heat and keep warm.

Lay the tortillas out on a flat surface. Divide the kimchi rice between them, then place the tofu on top. Spoon over some black beans, add a few slices of avocado, and top with tomato and baby spinach. Roll the burrito closed and drizzle with soured cream.

# MEAT & SEA FOOD

Korea is a peninsula, and thus the farmers harvest from both the land and the sea in great bounty. The sweeping popularity of Korean barbecue has made the country most lauded for its mastery of beef, but Korea has a deep love for seafood as well... and so do I!

# Grilled Beef Short Ribs

## Wang Galbi Gui

*Galbi, beef short ribs, is one of the most loved cuts of Korean barbecue. Nicely marbled and full of flavour, everyone loves this sweet–salty meat boasting a heady mix of garlic and ginger. Serve this cut in the traditional Korean way, with ssam leaves to wrap and ssamjang sauce. You'll quickly see why this dish is so popular.*

**Serves 4**

1.2kg (2lb 10oz) beef short ribs
  (with bone)
3 tbsp garlic, grated or finely chopped
4 tsp ginger, peeled and grated
70ml (2¾fl oz) mirin
300ml (10fl oz) soy sauce
4 tbsp roasted sesame oil
2 tbsp brown sugar
1 pear, peeled and grated
½ tsp ground black pepper
vegetable oil, for frying
4 baby leeks or spring onions, trimmed
1 red onion, quartered
10–12 kkwari-gochu (shishito peppers)
  or padron peppers

TO SERVE
ssam leaves
Ssamjang Sauce (page 14)
Spring Onion Salad (page 147)
gim (roasted seaweed)
steamed short grain rice

Ask your butcher to give you short ribs cut into about 7.5cm (3in) lengths through the bone. Butterfly the meat into a long strip, keeping the meat attached to the rib. Score the meat in a criss cross pattern, along the full length of the meat.

For the marinade, in a large bowl, whisk together the garlic, ginger, mirin, soy sauce, sesame oil, sugar, pear and black pepper. Place the beef into a shallow dish or a food-safe plastic bag and tip in the marinade, making sure all of the meat is covered in the marinade. Marinate the beef for at least 1 hour or overnight in the fridge.

Heat a grill or griddle pan up over high heat and, once hot, brush the griddle lightly with vegetable oil. Shake off the excess marinade and place the beef under the grill or in the pan. Cook until charred and to the desired doneness (about 1 minute on each side for medium rare). Place the vegetables on the pan and cook until wilted and charred.

Use kitchen scissors to cut the beef into 2.5cm (1in) wide pieces and serve immediately alongside the ssam leaves, ssamjang sauce, spring onion salad, gim and rice.

# Galbi Steak Pie

*Steak pies are ubiquitous in Britain, and I have grown to relish these dense pastry parcels packed with meat, sometimes eaten cold. So I created this Galbi version that is a cross between American pot pies and the English pies I have had in London. It turned out so well – a richer, thicker, more savoury version of Galbijjim, a Korean short rib stew, kicked up with Guinness beer!*

**Serves 2–4**

700g (1lb 9oz) short ribs of beef,
 cut into 2.5cm (1in) cubes
50g (2oz) plain flour,
 plus extra for dusting
25g (1oz) butter
vegetable oil
2 medium onions, cut into 3cm (1¼in) dice
1 tsp ginger, grated
1 tsp garlic, grated
150ml (5fl oz) Guinness beer
120ml (4fl oz) soy sauce
3 tbsp mirin
1 tbsp roasted sesame oil
2 tbsp brown sugar
300ml (10fl oz) beef stock
185g (6½oz) baby potatoes
2 large carrots, peeled, halved lengthways
 and cut into half moons
175g (6oz) mixed mushrooms,
 halved if large
1 tsp freshly ground black pepper
1 egg
275g (10oz) puff pastry
sea salt

Coat the steak cubes in the flour and set aside.

In a heavy-based pan set over a medium–high heat, melt the butter and add a drizzle of oil. Add the onions, ginger and garlic and cook until softened and lightly golden brown. Place the steak in the pan and sear on all sides until browned. Drain any excess oil from the pan, and add the Guinness, soy sauce, mirin, sesame oil, sugar and beef stock. Bring to the boil. Add the potatoes, carrots and mushrooms, lower the heat to a simmer and cook for a further 1½ hours until the meat is very tender. Add the black pepper and season with salt to taste. Allow to cool completely.

Preheat the oven to 170°C fan/190°C/375°F/gas 5. Spoon the mixture into a 900ml (1¾ pint) dolsot bowl, or another ovenproof dish.

Crack the egg in a small bowl, add a splash of water and beat well to make an egg wash.

Roll out the puff pastry to a 3mm (⅛in) thick round, about 1cm (½in) wider than the bowl or dish, moisten rim of dish with the egg wash, and place the pastry on top, sealing the edges well. Cut away any excess pastry and brush with egg wash. If you wish, add any decorative touches with the pastry trimmings and brush with egg wash. Bake for 1–1½ hours until the pastry is golden brown and the filling is hot.

# Turkey Sausage Roll

*I live near the famous Ginger Pig butchers in London, and I often buy their sausage rolls on Sunday mornings on my way to Regent's Park. This recipe is a healthier version using lean turkey meat, infused with delicate Korean aromatics to pack it full of flavour.*

**Serves 4-6**

600g (1lb 5oz) turkey mince

3 tbsp soy sauce

2 tsp mirin

2 tsp roasted sesame oil

1 tsp ginger, peeled and grated

4 tsp shallot, finely diced

1 tsp garlic, grated

2 tsp roasted sesame seeds

1 tsp chives, finely chopped

2 tsp gyeoja (Korean mustard)

2 tsp dwengjang
  (Korean soy bean paste)

1 tsp gochujang
  (Korean chilli paste)

1 egg, beaten

160g (5¾oz) puff pastry

plain flour, for dusting

1 tsp black and white sesame seeds

sea salt and freshly ground black pepper

Gochujang Mustard or Gochujang
  Mayonnaise (page 14), to serve

Preheat the oven to 180°C fan/200°C/400°F/gas 6.

In a large bowl, mix together the turkey, soy sauce, mirin, sesame oil, ginger, shallot, garlic, sesame seeds, chives, gyeoja, dwengjang and gochujang, and season well with salt and pepper to taste. Set aside.

In a small bowl, make an egg wash by lightly beating the egg with a splash of water. Set aside.

Roll the puff pastry out on a floured surface to a rectangle 30cm x 35cm (12 x 14in) wide, and 3mm (⅛in) thick.

Scoop the turkey out of the bowl and form a thick log across the width of the puff pastry, just below the centre line. Brush beaten egg across the bottom edge of the pastry. Fold the top edge of the pastry over onto the egg-washed edge, and gently press down. Crimp the edge with a fork to seal. Egg wash the top of the roll and add any decorations using the pastry scraps. Sprinkle the sesame seeds on top.

Place the sausage roll onto a baking sheet lined with parchment paper, and cook for 45 minutes, or until the turkey is cooked through and the pastry is crisp and golden. Check the core temperature using a thermometer – it should read 75°C (167°F). Allow to cool slightly, then cut into pieces. Serve with gochujang mustard or gochujang mayonnaise.

# Beef Bulgogi

*Bulgogi literally means 'fire meat' as it is traditionally cooked over a grill at the table. You can buy thinly sliced bulgogi meat at Korean grocers, but it is hard to control the quality, so I find it best to thinly slice your favourite cut of beef instead. I like using rib eye, as it is so flavourful and has nice marbling. I prefer to cook bulgogi in a pan, rather than on a grill, to capture the tasty juices that are released from the meat – so good on rice!*

**Serves 3–4**

450g (1lb) (about 2 large) rib eye beef
  steaks, trimmed
1 onion, thinly sliced
2 spring onions, thinly sliced at an angle
vegetable oil, for frying

MARINADE
5 garlic cloves, grated
2 tsp ginger, grated
1½ tsp mirin
140ml (4¾fl oz) soy sauce
2 tbsp roasted sesame oil
2 tsp brown sugar
3½ tbsp apple juice
⅛ tsp freshly ground black pepper

TO SERVE
steamed short grain rice
ssam leaves
Spicy Pickled Radishes (page 47)

Wrap the rib eye steaks in clingfilm and place in the freezer for about 2 hours, to partially freeze the meat. Remove from the freezer and unwrap and thinly slice the meat to about 2mm (⅛in) thick (or as thin as possible). Place in a shallow dish and set aside.

In a medium bowl, whisk together the marinade ingredients, making sure the sugar is dissolved. Tip into the beef dish, and mix to coat the meat entirely, gently massaging the marinade in. Allow to marinate for 2 hours or overnight in the fridge.

In a non-stick frying pan placed over a medium–high heat, drizzle a little vegetable oil to lightly coat the bottom of the pan. Tip in the beef and all of the marinade. Stir in the onions and cook for about 3 minutes until the beef is just medium rare and the onions are softened. Remove from the heat and stir in the spring onions. Serve immediately with rice, ssam leaves and the pickled radishes.

# Rib-Eye Steak with Signature Sauces

*At my restaurant we often serve steaks with Korean-inspired sauces and butters. The kimchi
béarnaise is my ultimate favourite – a rich, creamy sauce mixed with the tang and spice of kimchi.
I also love the unique twist on chimichurri using fragrant perilla leaves, lifting this spirited garlicky
chilli dressing with style. The bulgogi butter is an umami bomb, and so fabulous on a perfectly
charred steak, melting into the crevices. Serve any of these toppings with your choice cut of steak.*

## Serves 4

4 x 200g (7oz) rib eye steaks, at room
temperature
vegetable oil, for cooking

PERILLA LEAF CHIMICHURRI
6 perilla leaves, finely chopped
½ tsp oregano, chopped
2 tsp garlic, grated
juice of 1 lime
50g (2oz) shallots, finely chopped
50g (2oz) jalapeños, deseeded and finely
chopped
170ml (6fl oz) extra virgin olive oil
2 tbsp white wine vinegar
sea salt and freshly ground black pepper

BULGOGI BUTTER
3 tbsp soy sauce
3 tsp white sugar
3 tsp light brown sugar
1 tbsp gochugaru (Korean chilli flakes)
2 garlic cloves, roughly chopped
2.5cm (1in) piece of ginger, peeled and
roughly chopped
250g (9oz) unsalted butter, at room
temperature
1 spring onion, finely chopped
a pinch of freshly ground black pepper

KIMCHI BÉARNAISE
3 tbsp sagwa-shikcho (Korean apple vinegar)
½ tbsp shallots, finely chopped
125g (4oz) unsalted butter
3 large egg yolks
5 tsp liquid from kimchi
50g (2oz) cabbage kimchi, finely chopped
1½ tbsp chives, finely chopped

To make the chimichurri, put the perilla leaves, oregano, garlic, lime
juice, shallots and jalapeños in a bowl. Mix well, and pour in the oil and
vinegar, whisking well together. Season with salt and pepper to taste.

For the bulgogi butter, combine the soy sauce and sugars in a small
saucepan. Simmer for a few minutes until thickened. Leave to cool to
room temperature. Once cool, put the gochugaru, garlic and ginger
in a food processor and pulse until finely chopped. Add the softened
butter and blend until smooth and evenly mixed. With the motor
running, slowly pour in the cooled soy mix until smooth. Scoop into
a bowl and mix in the chopped spring onion and black pepper.

Lay out a couple of large sheets of clingfilm about 25cm (10in) in
length and spoon the butter down the middle to roughly form a
2.5cm (1in) thick log. Wrap the clingfilm around the butter tightly
and twist the ends to seal. Refrigerate until needed.

For the béarnaise, place the sagwa-shikcho and shallots in a small
saucepan over a medium-high heat and reduce the sagwa-shikcho
until roughly 1 tablespoon remains. Set aside to cool completely.

Place the butter in a small, heavy-based saucepan over a low heat
until the butter has melted then pour into a measuring jug. Place the
sagwa-shikcho and shallot mixture, egg yolks and liquid from the
kimchi in the bowl of a food processor. Blend the ingredients together
and, whilst the blender is running, slowly add the butter in a steady
stream until the mixture is thick and smooth. Fold in the chopped
kimchi and chives and season to taste.

Season both sides of the steaks well. Heat up a griddle pan over a high
heat; lightly brush the pan with oil. Cook the steaks, flipping once, until
done to your liking. Allow to rest for at least 15 minutes, then serve
with the sauce or butter of your choice.

# Chicken Kaesu Curry

## with Black Rice

*My sister used to make me curry and rice for dinner sometimes when we lived together in New York. Admittedly, she did use Korean ready-made curry cubes that just dissolve with water, but making a homemade curry is so easy and tastes so much better. You'll never buy the cubes again! You can also add raw chicken into the curry sauce, to make chicken curry, if you prefer.*

**Serves 4**

4 skinless chicken breasts, pounded
vegetable oil, for frying
1 tsp garlic, grated
300g (11oz) baby onions or
    shallots, peeled and cut in half
2 carrots, peeled and cut at an angle
480ml (16fl oz) chicken stock
450ml (15fl oz) Dashi Stock (page 29)
200g (7oz) baby potatoes, cut in half
60g (2oz) plain flour
60g (2oz) butter
2 tbsp madras curry powder
½ tbsp ginger, grated
70g (2¾oz) sugar snap peas,
    trimmed
1 tbsp sea salt flakes
sea salt freshly ground black pepper

PANÉ BATTER
80g (3oz) plain flour
2 large eggs, beaten
100g (3½oz) panko breadcrumbs

TO SERVE
cooked black rice
pickled ginger

Season the chicken breasts evenly with salt and pepper, place on a rack in the fridge and leave to brine for 6 hours, or overnight for the best results.

Drizzle a little oil into a heavy-based saucepan and add the garlic and onions. Sauté for 2–3 minutes until softened. Add the carrot and sauté for about 3 minutes until slightly softened. Add the chicken stock and dashi stock and bring to a simmer. Add the potatoes and cook for 15–20 minutes until tender. Remove from the heat and set aside.

In a medium saucepan, make a roux: toast the flour over a medium-high heat until browned, stirring constantly. Add the butter and stir in the curry powder and ginger. Cook for 3 minutes. Remove from the heat and tip the butter curry mixture into the pan with the carrot, potatoes and stock mixing the curry well into the broth. Bring to a simmer and cook for 4–5 minutes until thickened. Add the sugar snap peas and cook for about 2 minutes until just softened. Add the salt.

Half fill a heavy-based saucepan with oil and heat to 180°C (350°F).

Place the flour, egg and breadcrumbs in three separate shallow bowls. Dredge the chicken breasts in the flour, then dip in the egg, and finally coat them in panko breadcrumbs. Place a chicken breast carefully into the oil, and fry, flipping once during cooking. The chicken is done when the thickest part registers 75°C (167°F) on a meat thermometer. Place on a wire rack and keep warm in a low oven, and repeat until all of the chicken is cooked.

Place the chicken breasts on a chopping board and cut into 2cm (¾in) thick strips. Serve on black rice and spoon the curry on top, with a side of pickled ginger.

# Spicy Pork Belly Stir-Fry

*This quick and easy stir-fry is so incredibly tasty it will become one of your go-to dishes. You can use any cut of pork, but I like the combination of shoulder and belly to get a nice mix of meaty and fatty flavour. The spicy marinade is lip-smackingly good as well. Serve on top of rice to soak up all of the sauce.*

## Serves 2

250g (9oz) boneless pork shoulder, trimmed and cut into 2.5cm (1in) cubes
250g (9oz) pork belly, trimmed and cut into 4cm (1½in) thick x 1cm (½in) thick pieces
vegetable oil, for frying
4 tbsp soju (Korean spirit)
½ large onion, thinly sliced
½ large carrot, peeled and thinly sliced at an angle
120g (3¾oz) white cabbage, cut into 2.5cm (1in) cubes
8 perilla leaves, cut into 1 cm (½in) pieces
¼ tsp salt

MARINADE
2 tbsp gochugaru (Korean chilli flakes)
1 tbsp gochujang (Korean chilli paste)
2 tbsp soy sauce
1 tbsp mirin
3 tbsp apple juice
2 tsp roasted sesame oil
1 tsp garlic, grated or finely chopped
½ tsp ginger, peeled and grated
a good pinch of freshly ground black pepper

TO SERVE
cooked rice
1 tsp roasted sesame seeds
a drizzle of roasted sesame oil
2 spring onions, thinly sliced at an angle

In a medium bowl, stir together all the ingredients for the marinade along with 2 tablespoons of water. Add both types of pork and toss to coat. Allow to marinate at room temperature for about 30 minutes or cover and refrigerate overnight.

In a medium frying pan, add a drizzle of vegetable oil and heat over a medium–high heat. Add the pork and all of the marinade, and cook for 5 minutes, stirring occasionally, until the meat is cooked through, golden and lightly caramelized in areas. Add the soju to dissolve any browned bits left in the pan and flavour the sauce. Add the onion, carrot, cabbage and salt and cook for 3–4 minutes more, stirring occasionally, until the vegetables have softened and are cooked through. Once the vegetables are cooked, remove from the heat and stir in the perilla leaves.

Serve immediately over rice, sprinkle with roasted sesame seeds, a drizzle of sesame oil, and spring onion slices to finish.

# KFC Wings

*Korean fried chicken has been the rage around the world as of late. The extra crispy crust makes it so different and addictive compared to other fried chicken. My secret ingredient is matzo meal, a Jewish unleavened flatbread, which keeps this crust super crunchy. And a splash of vodka, which prevents gluten development, making these wings cracking.*

**Makes 24–26 pieces**

60g (2½oz) sea salt, plus an extra ⅛ tsp
2 tsp whole black peppercorns
juice and zest of 1 lemon
25g (1 oz) ginger, peeled and roughly chopped
7 garlic cloves, roughly chopped
½ white onion, roughly chopped
2 leeks, white part only, roughly chopped
1½ tbsp dwengjang (Korean soy bean paste)
1.3 kg (3lb) chicken wings, cut into drumettes and wingettes (discard or reserve the tips for another use)
90g (3¼oz) cornflour
⅛ tsp freshly ground black pepper
vegetable oil, for frying

SWEET AND SPICY CHILLI SAUCE:
110g (3¾oz) gochujang (Korean chilli paste)
2 tbsp soy sauce
1½ tbsp rice wine vinegar
100g (3½oz) dark brown sugar
2 garlic cloves, grated or finely chopped
2.5cm (1in) piece ginger, peeled and grated
1 tbsp roasted sesame oil

BATTER
140g (4½oz) cornflour
70g (2¾oz) fine matzo meal
70g (2¾oz) plain flour
3 tbsp gochugaru (Korean chilli flakes)
1 tbsp sea salt
3 tbsp garlic powder
3 tbsp onion powder
½ tsp baking powder
150ml (5fl oz) vodka

TO SERVE
roasted white sesame seeds, to sprinkle
spring onion, finely sliced at an angle
Sweet and Spicy Chilli Sauce
Sweet Soy Sauce (page 77)

First make the spicy chilli sauce. Combine all of the ingredients in a small saucepan set over a medium–low heat and whisk well. Bring to the boil, stirring constantly to prevent burning. Cook for about 4 minutes then remove from the heat and set aside.

For the brine, add 250ml (8fl oz) water to a large saucepan and add the 60g (2½oz) sea salt, black peppercorns, lemon zest and juice, ginger, garlic, onion, leeks and dwengjang. Bring this to a low simmer and stir until the salt and dwengjang have dissolved. Remove from the heat and let it cool completely. When the liquid is cool, add another 750ml (26fl oz) water. Submerge the chicken wings in the brine, and place into the fridge. After 24 hours, remove from the brine and pat dry. Discard the brine.

To make the pre-coating, in a large bowl mix together the cornflour, the ⅛ teaspoon salt and the freshly ground black pepper. Add the chicken and toss well until evenly coated all over. Shake off the excess, and transfer the chicken to a rack.

Half fill a heavy-based saucepan with oil and heat to 190°C (375°F).

To make the batter, in a large bowl whisk together all of the dry ingredients. In a smaller bowl, whisk together 475ml (16fl oz) water and the vodka. Just before frying, whisk the wet mixture little by little into the dry mixture. You may not need all of the liquid: the consistency should be relatively thin and runny.

Working in batches, use tongs to dip each piece of chicken into the batter, letting any excess batter drip off. Hold the chicken pieces in the hot oil for a few seconds to seal before releasing them, to prevent them from sticking to the bottom of the pan. Fry until golden crispy brown and the thickest part registers 75°C (167°F) on a meat thermometer. Keep the cooked chicken warm in a low oven until all batches are done.

Sprinkle the chicken with sesame seeds and spring onion and drizzle with sweet soy sauce and sweet chilli sauce, or serve on the side.

# Pan-Fried Flounder

## Saengseon Jeon

*I remember watching my mom make this delicate fish dish for special occasions and parties. She used a large electric flat griddle pan that only came out when she was making jeon. Watching her tip the fish from the flour, to the egg, and then frying it so carefully so as not to lose the lovely yellow colour, but making it crispy, was wondrous. She still makes this for me when I come home to visit New Jersey.*

**Serves 4**

40g (1½oz) rice flour
1 egg, beaten with a pinch of salt
4 fillets of boneless, skinless flounder, flat fish
  or red snapper
4 garlic chives, cut to the same length as
  the fish fillets
vegetable oil, for frying
sea salt and freshly ground black pepper
Pancake Dipping Sauce (page 14), to serve

Put the rice flour and beaten egg into separate wide, shallow bowls. Season the fish lightly with salt and pepper and set aside for about 5 minutes to allow the seasonings to soak in. Lightly dredge the fish in the flour, tapping off any excess.

In a large non-stick frying pan, heat 2 tablespoons of oil over a medium heat. Working in batches, coat the fish in the egg, letting any excess drip into the bowl, and place into the frying pan. Press a chive down the middle of each piece of fish. Cook for about 4 minutes until golden brown, flipping halfway through.

Transfer to a wire rack or kitchen paper-lined plate to drain. Repeat with the remaining fish, adding more oil to the pan as needed.

Transfer the fish to a platter and serve immediately with the dipping sauce.

# Pan-fried Salmon with Green Chilli Glaze

*This green chilli glaze has popped up on the menu at my restaurants in various forms. It's a divine mix of sweet soy with a complex chilli kick at the end. The richness of salmon goes brilliantly with the sauce, complemented with a fresh spring onion salad, and fragrant yuja pickles. Do try this sauce on other seafood, chicken and beef.*

**Serves 4**

4 skinless salmon fillets, about
  100g (3½oz) each
vegetable oil, for frying

GREEN CHILLI GLAZE
150ml (5fl oz) soy sauce
110g (3¾oz) brown sugar
4 tbsp rice wine vinegar
3 garlic cloves, finely chopped
60g (2½oz) jalapeños or large green
  chillies, finely chopped
4 tbsp vegetable oil
2½ tbsp roasted sesame oil

SPRING ONION SALAD
(PA MUCHIM)
4 tsp soy sauce
1½ tbsp rice wine vinegar
2 tsp gochugaru (Korean chilli flakes)
½ tbsp roasted sesame oil
1 tsp roasted sesame seeds
1 tsp white sugar
4 spring onions, trimmed

TO SERVE
1 green chilli, finely sliced
2 tsp silgochu (dried chilli threads)
120g (3¾oz) yuja pickles
cooked rice

First make the green chilli glaze: in a small bowl, whisk together the soy sauce, sugar, vinegar and 4 tablespoons water. Set aside.

In a small non-stick frying pan, sauté the garlic and the jalapeños with the vegetable oil until softened. Tip in the soy sauce mixture and stir well, making sure the sugar is fully dissolved. Simmer until reduced by half. Once reduced, remove from the heat and add the sesame oil. Set aside in a warm place.

Next make the spring onion salad: in a small bowl, whisk together the soy sauce, vinegar, gochugaru, sesame oil, sesame seeds and sugar. Whisk well until the sugar is dissolved. Set aside.

Cut the spring onions into 5cm (2in) lengths and julienne into thin strips. Soak in ice-cold water for about 5 minutes until crisp and curly. Drain and dry.

In a large non-stick frying pan placed over a medium–high heat, drizzle a generous amount of vegetable oil. Once the oil is hot, add the salmon fillets – do not overcrowd the pan, and work in batches if necessary. Cook the salmon for 3–4 minutes, then flip over and cook for a further 3–4 minutes until the salmon is slightly golden brown and cooked to your taste.

Place the spring onions in a large bowl, drizzle over the spring onion dressing, and toss to coat.

Place the salmon on plates, spoon over the green chilli glaze, and garnish with the spring onion salad and green chilli slices. Top with a pinch of silgochu and serve with yuja pickles, rice and the rest of the spring onion salad.

# Oysters with Kimchi Granita

*I love raw oysters and am guilty of dousing them in an offensive amount of hot sauce.
Here, spice comes forth in the form of a refreshing kimchi granita. The tang and spice
from the kimchi marries so well with the brine of oysters, and adds gorgeous colour.*

**Makes 12 oysters**

½ tsp yuja (yuzu) juice

½ tsp white sugar

100ml (3½fl oz) liquid from kimchi, passed
through a fine sieve

1 tsp sagwa-shikcho (Korean apple vinegar)

2 tsp cucumber juice

2 pinches of salt

12 fresh oysters, shucked on the half shell,
chilled

2 tbsp cucumber, very finely diced

2 tbsp shallots, very finely diced

4 chives, cut into 3cm (1¼in) lengths

4 lemon wedges, to serve

In a small bowl, add the yuja juice, sugar, kimchi liquid, vinegar,
cucumber juice and salt. Whisk well until all incorporated. Pour
into a small shallow glass baking dish and place in the freezer.
Freeze for 1 hour, then scrape with a fork, making shards (the
centre may still be slushy). Freeze for another hour and scrape
again with a fork, breaking apart the crystals. Repeat another
2–3 times, until all is frozen and the granita is light and fluffy.
Keep in the freezer.

Place the oysters on a deep plate, securing with crushed ice.
Spoon a teaspoon of granita over each oyster and top with
cucumber, shallots and chives. Serve immediately with lemon
wedges.

# Grilled Mussels with Perilla and Cheese

## Honghap Gui

*Although this recipe may not seem Korean per se, this is a dish that I have enjoyed many times in various forms while visiting the seaside towns there. Large penshell mussels are local to Korean shores (think of a mussel the size of your shoe), and restaurants will just throw them straight on the grill in the half-shell. The shell acts as a dish, and all kinds of delicious ingredients get thrown in, with cheese, bacon and sweetcorn being the most popular. Here, I have used common mussels – and go crazy with Tabasco, the more the better!*

**Serves 4 as starter**

900g (2lb) mussels, cleaned and
    debearded
110g (3¾oz) salted butter
3 tbsp garlic, grated
3 tbsp perilla leaves, finely chopped
50g (2oz) mature Cheddar cheese, finely
    grated
25g (1oz) Parmesan, grated
20g (¾oz) panko breadcrumbs
5–6 dashes of Tabasco

Place the mussels in a steaming basket in the bottom of a large, deep pan. Fill with water until just touching the bottom of the basket, and bring to the boil. Steam the mussels for about 3–4 minutes just until opened.

Discard any mussels that haven't opened then remove and discard the top shells from the open mussels. Line the mussels up on a foil-lined baking sheet, open side up.

In a small saucepan, melt the butter over a low heat, add the garlic and cook for 2–3 minutes until softened, but not browned. Remove from the heat and mix in the perilla leaves.

Preheat the oven to 180°C fan/200°C/400°F/gas 6.

In a medium bowl, mix together the cheeses and panko breadcrumbs.

Spoon a little of the butter, garlic and perilla mixture into each mussel shell. Sprinkle the cheese panko mixture on top.

Bake for about 5–6 minutes until the cheese is melted and the panko is golden brown. Drizzle with Tabasco as you prefer. Serve immediately.

# Braised Mackerel with Radish

## Godeungeo Mu Jorim

*My mom used to cook mackerel often, and this dish is based on her recipe. She used to use canned mackerel when she could not find fresh fish, and it still tasted great. Serve with multigrain rice and this dish becomes a very healthy and satisfying meal.*

**Serves 2**

2 mackerel fillets, skin on
200g (7oz) mu (Korean white radish) or mooli, peeled and cut into 3cm (1¼in) squares, 1cm (½in) thick

SAUCE
1 medium leek, white part only, thinly sliced at an angle
3 tbsp soy sauce
4 tbsp Dashi Stock (page 29) or water
1 tsp brown sugar
1 tbsp gochugaru (Korean chilli flakes)
1 tsp garlic, grated
2 tsp roasted sesame oil

Rinse the mackerel fillets in cold water and cut each fillet in half. Set aside.

Bring a medium pan, half filled with water, to the boil. Blanch the mu for 30 seconds. Remove and refresh under cold running water to halt the cooking process.

To make the sauce, mix all the ingredients together; set aside.

Place the squares of mu in the bottom of a heavy-based pan, layering them up if necessary. Place the four pieces of mackerel on top. Spoon the sauce on the top of the mackerel liberally.

Cover with a lid, place the pan over a low-medium heat and bring to a simmer. Once simmering, baste the mackerel with the sauce, and add warm water as necessary to prevent burning. Cook for about 20 minutes until the radishes are soft and the mackerel is cooked through. Serve with multigrain rice.

# SOUP &NOO DLES

Korea's bitterly cold winters have yielded a rich tradition of warming soups and stews. Often served still bubbling to the table, these bowls are full of deep flavour and offer wide variety. Noodles are also of note, whether hand-cut or torn, made from sweet potatoes or buckwheat, or served hot or cold. You'll surely find something to satisfy any hankering.

# Banquet Noodles with Clams

## Janchi Guksu

*This dish, which literally translates as 'feast' or 'banquet' noodles, is often associated with marriage, with the noodles symbolizing longevity. This light, yet so incredibly flavourful broth is divine – clean and rejuvenating. I've added clams to give this special occasion dish an added layer of luxury.*

**Serves 2**

500g (1lb 2oz) clams, cleaned
2 rainbow carrots, peeled and julienned
1 hobak (Korean courgette), julienned
a pinch of salt
2 large eggs, lightly beaten
180g (6¼oz) somyeon noodles
  (Korean wheat flour noodles)
4 yubu (Korean fried tofu), cut into strips

ANCHOVY STOCK

8 myulchi (large dried anchovies),
  heads and guts removed
13cm (5in) piece of dashima (dried kelp)
4 large garlic cloves, sliced
3cm (1¼in) thick slice of mu (Korean
  white radish) or mooli
3 tbsp soy sauce
2 tbsp fish sauce

For the stock, in a large pan, combine the myulchi, dashima, garlic, mu, soy sauce, fish sauce and 2.3 litres (4 pints) water and bring to the boil over a high heat. Reduce the heat to a simmer and cook for 20 minutes. Pass the anchovy stock through a fine-mesh sieve into another large pan (or transfer to a bowl and return to the same pan) and discard the solids.

For the additions, return the stock to the boil over a high heat and cook the clams in the stock until they open, then remove and set aside. Blanch the carrots in the stock and remove using a slotted spoon, then repeat to blanch the hobak in the same way. Set the vegetables aside and keep the stock warm.

For the eggs, in a medium non-stick frying pan, heat a drizzle of oil over a medium heat. Beat the salt into the eggs, then pour the egg mixture into the pan, swirling to evenly coat the base. Cook, undisturbed, until the egg is set but just barely browned on the bottom, about 2 minutes. Flip and continue to cook for a further 15–20 seconds until the bottom is set, again trying not to get too much colour on the egg. Slide onto a chopping board, carefully roll into a log and cut crossways into thin strips. Set the egg strips aside.

For the noodles, bring a medium pan of water to the boil and add the noodles. When the water comes back to the boil, add a couple of spoons of cold water and cook according to packet instructions. Drain the noodles and shock in cold water to stop the cooking. Drain and rinse in cold water to remove any extra starch. Divide the noodles into two portions and place the mounds in a colander to drain.

Place the noodles into serving bowls and pour the hot broth over the top. Arrange half of the egg strips, yubu, carrots and hobak in each bowl and place the clams around the sides.

# Seafood Silken Tofu Soup

## Soon Dubu Jiggae

*This is by far my most favourite of all Korean soups and stews. All of my friends know this and joke with me that whenever I visit Seoul, it is the first meal that I have. I love fresh seafood in this bubbling pot, although there are many different versions to try. Shellfish works best, with whole prawns, clams and mussels adding the most flavour.*

**Serves 4**

½ onion, diced

2 tbsp gochugaru (Korean chilli flakes)

2 garlic cloves, grated or finely chopped

1 tsp ginger, peeled and grated

1 small courgette, halved lengthways and cut into 1cm (½in) slices

150g (5oz) assorted mushrooms (button, enoki, oyster, shiitake), stems removed and sliced

100g (3½oz) Korean or Chinese cabbage leaves, thickly sliced

400g (14oz) silken tofu, drained

4 jumbo prawns, cleaned

720g (1lb 9oz) clams, cleaned

560g (1lb 4oz) mussels, cleaned and debearded

4 scallops

1 large egg

sea salt and freshly ground black pepper

STOCK

½ onion, roughly chopped

4 dried shiitake mushrooms

1 spring onion, roughly chopped

13cm (5in) piece of dashima (dried kelp)

8 myulchi (large dried anchovies), heads and guts removed

TO SERVE

roasted sesame oil

handful of chives, cut into 7.5cm (3in) lengths

steamed short grain rice

To make the stock, combine the onion, dried mushrooms, spring onion, dashima, myulchi and 750ml (26fl oz) water in a large pan and bring to the boil over a high heat. Reduce the heat to a simmer and cook, covered, for about 45 minutes. Strain, discarding the solids, and set aside.

In a medium heavy-based pan, heat a drizzle of vegetable oil over a medium–low heat. Add the onion and gochugaru and cook for 5 minutes, stirring occasionally, until the onion is softened. Stir in the garlic and ginger, add the stock and bring to a simmer over a medium–high heat.

Add the courgette, fresh mushrooms and cabbage and bring to the boil. Reduce the heat to a simmer and cook for 2 minutes, until the vegetables are slightly softened. Carefully add the tofu in chunks, season with salt and gently stir, keeping the tofu intact as much as possible. Place all the seafood on top and cover with the lid. Cook for a further 5 minutes. When the clams and mussels have opened and the prawns have turned a pink colour, crack an egg into the pan and gently mix it into the stew so that it begins to poach in the hot liquid. Discard any clams or mussels that haven't opened.

Remove the stew from the heat and top with a drizzle of sesame oil and a sprinkle of chives. Serve in bowls with the steamed rice on the side.

# Korean Spicy Cold Noodles with Squid

## Bibim Naengmyun

*My father was born in what is now North Korea, and this dish from the region is one of his favourites. This spicy bowl is a popular variation to the more known mild, tangy, soupy version. I have topped it off with some grilled squid which goes gorgeously with the fiery sweet sauce.*

**Serves 2**

4 baby squid, cleaned
vegetable oil, for cooking
200g (7oz) nokcha naengmyun
  (Korean green tea buckwheat noodles)
sea salt

CHILLI SAUCE
2 tbsp gochugaru (Korean chilli flakes)
1 tbsp gochujang (Korean chilli paste)
1 tbsp soy sauce
2 tbsp sagwa-shikcho
  (Korean apple vinegar)
1 tbsp caster sugar
2 tsp honey
½ tsp garlic, finely grated
1 tbsp plum extract
½ tsp roasted sesame seeds, crushed
1 tsp roasted sesame oil
½ spring onion, green part only,
  finely sliced at an angle

TO SERVE
3 breakfast radishes, thinly sliced and
  soaked in ice-cold water
2 pinches silgochu (dried chilli threads)
1 quail egg, soft boiled, peeled and halved
daikon radish cress

First make the sauce: in a small bowl, whisk together all the ingredients. Place in the fridge and leave to mellow.

Cut the squid bodies into rings and any large tentacles in half. Drizzle a bit of vegetable oil into a non-stick griddle pan, placed over a medium–high heat. Add the squid and grill for 2–3 minutes until the squid is tender and just cooked through. Season with salt to taste.

Cook the nokcha naengmyun according to the packet instructions. Rinse well with cold water, massaging to remove excess starch. Drain and set aside.

Divide the nokcha naengmyun between two bowls. Top the noodles with the radishes. Divide the chargrilled squid between the bowls. Finish with a pinch of silgochu, half an egg and daikon cress in each bowl. Serve immediately with the chilli sauce on the side.

# Japchae with Uni and Oysters

*Japchae, seasoned sweet potato noodles, is a much loved dish, usually made with vegetables and beef. This dazzling version boasts gems of the sea – sea urchin and oysters, tossed in a vibrant, bright citrus–soy dressing. Finish it off with a hint of bottarga and this is one of the most lavish versions of japchae you'll ever taste. Do find the freshest sea urchin you can, as the quality makes a huge difference in this dish. I prefer the ones from Japan or Santa Barbara, California.*

## Serves 2

160g (5¼oz) japchae noodles (sweet potato noodles), cooked according to packet instructions (cooked weight 500g (1lb 2oz))
30g (1oz) unsalted butter
2 tsp shallots, finely chopped
8 oysters, shucked
½ bunch enoki mushrooms, trimmed
2 tbsp soy sauce
2 tsp yuja (yuzu) juice
handful garlic chives, cut into 3cm (1¼in) lengths
1 tsp roasted sesame seeds
6 pieces raw uni (sea urchin)
1 tsp red tobiko (flying fish roe)
1–2 tsp bottarga, grated
omelette, cut into 2mm (⅛in) strips (page 157)
1 tsp nori, shredded (optional)
sea salt and freshly ground black pepper

Cook the sweet potato noodles according to the packet instructions. Rinse with warm water and set aside.

Place a non-stick frying pan over a medium–low heat. Toss in the butter and, when melted, add the shallots and sauté for 2–3 minutes until softened. Add the oysters and cook for a further 2–3 minutes until just firm, then add the enoki mushrooms and sauté for an additional 2–3 minutes until wilted.

Add the sweet potato noodles, soy sauce and yuja juice to the pan. Break apart the noodles carefully with chopsticks or tongs, mixing to coat entirely with the sauce. Cook until the noodles are heated through and glossy, then toss in the garlic chives and sesame seeds. Season with salt and pepper to taste.

Divide the noodles between two plates, and top each with three pieces of fresh raw uni and half of the tobiko. Finish with grated bottarga and egg strips. Serve immediately.

# Noodles in Cold Bean Soup

## Kong Guksu

*My aunt in Korea served me this cold noodle bean soup in Busan when I was staying with her. I still remember tasting the salty, savoury chilled soup, mixed with toothsome, chewy handmade noodles. It has been one of my most loved summer soups since.*

**Serves 2**

360g (12¾oz) yeon dubu (silken tofu)
2 x 400g (14oz) cans organic black beans
  (with no added salt or sugar), drained
1 tbsp toasted pine nuts
2 tsp sea salt
200ml (7fl oz) unsweetened soy milk
  (optional)

NOODLES
500g (1lb 2oz) plain flour or strong flour,
  plus extra for dusting
½ tsp sea salt

TO SERVE
1 golden beetroot, thinly sliced
½ purple kohlrabi, thinly sliced
½ cucumber, julienned
1 tbsp edamame beans, pods and skins
  removed
2 tsp toasted pine nuts
sprinkle of black sesame seeds

For the noodles, put the flour and salt in a large bowl with 240ml (7¾fl oz) water. Stir together until a dough forms. Transfer to a clean work surface and knead for 10 minutes. The dough should feel very tough and should be able to easily lift from the work surface without sticking to it. Wrap the dough in clingfilm and rest in the fridge overnight.

For the soup, place the tofu, black beans, pine nuts and salt in a blender and process until smooth. If you prefer a thinner soup consistency, add the soy milk. Pour into a bowl and chill in the fridge.

Roll the noodle dough into a thin sheet on a floured surface. Dust the dough sheet with plenty of flour, then carefully roll up the sheet, and slice it into 5mm (¼in) thick noodles. Unfold the noodles and lightly shake off the excess flour.

To cook the noodles, bring a large pan of salted water to the boil over a medium–high heat. Add the noodles and immediately stir with chopsticks (or tongs), to prevent them sticking to the bottom. Cook the noodles for 3–4 minutes until they float to the surface of the water. Transfer to a colander and rinse quickly with cold water to cool.

Divide the noodles between two serving bowls. Pour in the chilled bean soup and arrange the beetroot, kohlrabi, cucumber, edamame beans, pine nuts and sesame seeds on top of the noodles to serve.

# Fish Chowder with Miso

*I have always loved my trips to New England and the bowls of hot chowder that inevitably arrive at the table. I've added just a few Korean twists to this classic recipe to make this warming bowl extraordinary. After the first bite, this chowder will become a regular request during the winter months.*

**Serves 2–4**

olive oil, for sautéing
40g (1½oz) butter
1 large banana shallot, finely diced
3 garlic cloves, grated
80g (3oz) bacon lardons
180ml (6¼fl oz) sake
1 litre (1¾ pints) chicken stock
2 tbsp mirin
1 tsp dwengjang
  (Korean soy bean paste)
2 tbsp white miso
200g (7oz) purple potato,
  diced into 1cm (½in) cubes
500g (1lb 2oz) cod fillets, cut into
  3 x 5cm (1¼ x 2in) pieces
500g (1lb 2oz) clams, cleaned
500g (1lb 2oz) mussels, cleaned
  and debearded
120g (3¾oz) frozen sweetcorn
½ red chilli, thinly sliced into rings
  at an angle (optional)
80g (3oz) baby spinach
2 spring onions, thinly sliced at an angle
sea salt and freshly ground black pepper

In a heavy-based pan, heat a drizzle of olive oil and the butter, and sauté the shallot and garlic until softened.

Add the lardons and cook for 3–4 minutes, stirring occasionally, until browned and the fat is rendered.

Add the sake to dissolve any browned bits from the bottom of the pan then increase the heat to high and bring to the boil. Add the chicken stock and mirin, then whisk in the dwengjang and miso until dissolved.

Add the diced potatoes and cod fillets, cook for 3–4 minutes, then add the clams and mussels. Cover and cook for a further 3–4 minutes until the shells are open. Discard any mussels that don't open. Remove the shells and return the mussel and clam meat to the chowder.

Add the sweetcorn, chilli, spinach and spring onions.
Mix and allow to simmer for another 3–4 minutes.
Season with salt and pepper to taste. Serve immediately.

# Kimchi Mac and Cheese

*Mac and cheese is probably one of the first dishes that I learned how to cook – albeit from a box with fluorescent coloured orange powder. It was so good, even cold! This recipe is definitely a strong upgrade from an instant version, with a béchamel base, four different types of cheese, and kicked up with a bit spice and crunch from the kimchi. Kimchi and cheese is a combination that is winning fans all around the world – at first bite you'll surely swoon and taste why.*

**Serves 6**

35g (1¼oz) salt
350g (12oz) dried elbow macaroni
75g (3oz) butter
20g (¾oz) plain flour
150ml (5fl oz) whole milk
400g (14oz) mixed cheese (blue, goat's, Cheddar, Parmesan), grated
450ml (15fl oz) double cream
250g (9oz) cabbage kimchi, chopped
chives, finely chopped, to serve

PANKO CRUST
50g (2oz) butter
100g (3½oz) panko breadcrumbs

Bring 3.5 litres (6 pints) water to the boil with the salt. Add the macaroni and cook until al dente. Drain well and set aside.

Preheat the oven to 70°C fan/90°C/200°F/gas ¼.

In a saucepan, melt the butter over a medium heat. Whisk in the flour and cook the mixture for just under 1 minute. Whisk in the milk, a little at a time, making sure to stir well so that no lumps form. Bring the mixture to the boil and cook for 10–15 minutes until you have a thickened and smooth sauce, whisking constantly.

Remove the sauce from the heat, add the cheese and cream, and stir until it is well combined and the cheese is melted, then add the chopped kimchi.

Add the macaroni to the sauce and mix well. Transfer to a deep suitably-sized ovenproof dish. Keep warm in the oven.

For the panko crust, melt the butter in a non-stick frying pan over a medium heat, then add the panko. Keep tossing and stirring until golden in colour. Remove the crumbs from the heat and sprinkle them evenly over the mac and cheese.

Scatter with chopped chives to finish and serve immediately.

# BREAD

Recently, Korea has had an insurgence
of French bakeries opening, and large
chains showcasing Asian-inspired bread
and pastries have popped up around the
country and the world. In this chapter,
I have taken some of my favourite recipes
and added a bit of Korean flare.

# Kimchi Cheese Pretzel Bites

*Having spent my formative years in New York City, I grew to love the ubiquitous NY pretzel sold on the streets. There is something so pleasing about this salty, chewy dough that I love. And, with kimchi and cheese stuffed in the middle, it just makes it even more irresistible. You won't be able to eat just one!*

## Makes 25 bites

365g (12¾oz) strong flour
1½ tsp salt
1 tbsp malt syrup
15g (½oz) fresh yeast (or 7g/¼oz dry yeast)
15g (½oz) unsalted butter, cut into small dice and softened
4 tbsp bicarbonate of soda
2 tbsp pretzel salt or 3 tbsp Cheddar cheese, grated or 2 tbsp black and white sesame seeds
Gochujang Mustard, to serve (page 14)

### KIMCHI AND CHEESE FILLING
15g (½oz) butter
200g (7oz) cabbage kimchi, chopped
120g (3¾oz) Parmesan, grated
100g (3½oz) Cheddar cheese, grated
freshly ground black pepper

For the filling, heat the butter in a medium frying pan and sauté the kimchi. Remove from the heat, put the kimchi into a bowl and allow to cool. Once cooled, add the grated cheese, mix thoroughly, and season. Divide the mixture into twenty-five portions and roll into balls. Place on a small tray and freeze for at least 2 hours.

To make the dough, combine the flour and salt in the bowl of a stand mixer fitted with a dough hook. In a small bowl, mix the malt syrup with 220ml (7¼fl oz) water, then add the yeast, whisking until fully incorporated. Add this to the mixer bowl and mix on low speed until blended. Add the butter pieces, increase the speed to medium and mix for about 8 minutes, until the dough has come together. Scrape the dough onto the work surface and divide it into twenty-five balls, about 25g (1oz) each. Place the balls on a lined tray, cover with clingfilm, and allow to rest for 15 minutes. Meanwhile, line two baking sheets and a tray with parchment paper.

Reshape the dough lightly. Gently flatten a ball, and place a frozen kimchi and cheese ball in the centre. Pinch the dough around the ball to enclose it. Reshape into a ball and place on the lined tray. Repeat with all of the dough and kimchi cheese balls. Once all of the pretzel bites are stuffed, cover with clingfilm and prove for 30 minutes.

Preheat the oven 180°C fan/200°C/400°F/gas 6. Shortly before baking, bring a large pan of water to the boil over a high heat and add the bicarbonate of soda. The mixture will be foamy at first, but the foam will dissipate. Carefully transfer a few pretzels to the simmering bicarbonate of soda. Working in batches of no more than five at a time, poach the pretzels for 30 seconds, then transfer with a slotted spoon to the lined baking sheets. Quickly sprinkle with the pretzel salt, grated cheese or sesame seeds, before they dry (so the topping sticks).

Bake the pretzel bites for 10-12 minutes until they become a chestnut brown colour, rotating the baking sheets halfway through. Remove from the oven and transfer to wire racks to cool slightly. Serve while still warm with gochujang mustard.

# Spring Onion and Cheese Waffles

*We serve these waffles at my restaurant with our Korean fried chicken for a great twist on the traditional 'Chicken & Waffles'. The green onions and cheese add great flavour, which is reminiscent of Chinese spring onion pancakes. The salty cheese also greatly complements the sweetness of the honey butter sauce.*

**Makes 10 waffles**

250g (9oz) plain flour
1 tbsp caster sugar
1 tbsp baking powder
1½ tsp mustard powder
½ tsp smoked paprika
1 tsp salt
1 tsp freshly ground black pepper
425ml (15fl oz) whole milk
115g (4oz) unsalted butter, melted
3 eggs
2 spring onions, finely chopped
3 tbsp garlic, grated
75g (3oz) Grana Padano, finely grated

HONEY BUTTER SAUCE
250g (9oz) butter, melted
4 garlic cloves, minced
175g (6oz) brown sugar
2½ tbsp soy sauce
2 tbsp honey

For the waffle batter, place the flour, sugar, baking powder, mustard powder, smoked paprika, salt and pepper in a large mixing bowl. Mix well.

In a second bowl, whisk the milk, melted butter and eggs together. Make a well in the dry mix, and pour the wet mixture into it. Whisk until fully blended and smooth, then whisk in the spring onions, garlic and cheese until well combined. Leave the batter to rest for 5 minutes (this is very important). Meanwhile, preheat a waffle maker.

Pour a ladleful of batter (about 100ml/3½fl oz) into the centre of each grid of the waffle maker. Close the lid and bake until golden brown and crispy on the outside: this should take around 3–4 minutes, depending on your waffle maker. Carefully open the lid and remove the waffle. Keep warm while you repeat with the remaining batter.

Next make the Honey Butter Sauce. In a small bowl, whisk together the melted butter, garlic, sugar, soy sauce and honey until fully incorporated and the sugar is dissolved.

Serve the waffles with the KFC Wings (page 143) and the honey butter sauce.

# Green Tea Monkey Bread

*I have been making monkey bread since I was in grade school. The green tea sugar adds not only great colour, but a wonderful sweet tea flavour that is perfect with this doughnut-like bread.*

**Serves 8–10**

250ml (8fl oz) whole milk

4 tbsp (1¾oz) granulated sugar

30g (1oz) unsalted butter, melted, plus extra for greasing

2 tsp vanilla extract with seeds

460g (1lb) plain flour, plus extra for dusting and flouring the pan

2¼ tsp rapid-rise or instant yeast

1 tsp salt

COATING

250g (9oz) white sugar

15g (½oz) green tea powder (matcha or garu nokcha)

115g (4oz) unsalted butter, melted

ICING

3 tbsp pasteurized egg whites

300g (11oz) icing sugar, sifted

1 tbsp yuja (yuzu) juice

3 tbsp pistachios, roughly chopped

Put the milk in a small saucepan with 125ml (4fl oz) water and warm to to 50˚C (122°F). Add the sugar, butter and vanilla and stir to combine.

In the bowl of an electric stand mixer fitted with a dough hook, combine the flour, yeast and salt. On a low speed, slowly add the milk mixture. Once the dough comes together, increase the speed to medium and mix for 7–8 minutes until shiny and smooth. Tip the dough onto a lightly floured work surface and knead it briefly to form a ball. Put the dough in a large bowl and cover with clingfilm. Place the bowl in a warm place until the dough doubles in size, about 1 hour.

While the dough is rising, mix the sugar and green tea powder for the coating in a small bowl and set aside. In another bowl, melt the butter and set aside. Grease a metal Bundt tin very generously with the butter, then dust with flour and set aside.

Turn the risen dough out onto a lightly floured surface. Pat the dough into a rough 20cm (8in) square, then cut into sixty-four 2.5cm (1in) square pieces. Roll each piece into a ball, dip in melted butter and roll in the sugar mixture, then layer into the prepared tin. Be sure to stagger the dough balls so they aren't stacked directly on top of each other; the staggering gives the bread the interlocking puzzle structure. Wrap the tin with clingfilm and let the dough rise until it is about 1.5cm (¾in) from the top of the tin, about 1 hour.

Preheat the oven to 175°C fan/195°C/375°F/gas 5. Once risen, remove the clingfilm and bake for about 35 minutes until the top is a deep brown. Leave to cool in the tin for 5 minutes, then turn out onto a wire rack.

For the icing, in the bowl of a stand mixer fitted with a paddle attachment, start beating the egg whites, then add the icing sugar 100g (3½oz) at a time, on medium-low speed. Add the yuja juice and beat until smooth. Drizzle the icing on top of the monkey bread generously and sprinkle with chopped pistachios.

# Korean Egg Bread

## Gyeran Bbang

*I love eating this 'egg bread' on the streets of Seoul. Usually, it is just made up of a pancake-like dough with egg. I have pimped out this version with some bacon, tomato and gooey cheese. I can see why it is such a popular street food, as it is so easy to eat on the go, yet still a completely gratifying breakfast.*

**Makes 9 egg breads**

250g (9oz) plain flour
2 tsp baking powder
½ tsp sea salt
250ml (8fl oz) whole milk
2 tsp butter, melted
2 eggs, beaten
15g (½oz) chives, chopped, to serve

TOPPING
9 egg yolks
120g (3¼oz) bacon, diced
90g (3oz) tomato, diced
120g (3¼oz) mozzarella cheese, grated
sea salt and freshly ground black pepper

Preheat the oven to 180°C fan/200°C/400°F/gas 6 and line a nine-hole muffin tin with paper cases.

For the batter, put the flour, baking powder, salt and pepper in a large bowl. Mix well.

In another bowl, whisk together the milk, butter and eggs.

Make a well in the centre of the dry mixture and pour the wet mixture into it. Gradually whisk it all together until fully blended and smooth.

Divide the mixture between the holes of the muffin tin and add an egg yolk to the top of each one. Sprinkle a little bacon, tomato, cheese and a pinch of salt over each one.

Bake the bread for 20–25 minutes, until set and golden brown. Sprinkle with chopped chives and serve immediately.

# DESS ERTS

I love infusing Korean ingredients into Western-style desserts. And this is probably my favourite chapter! You'll amaze your guests with these stunning, fun and unique desserts that will satiate your sweet tooth.

# Coconut Red Bean Misugaru Tiramisu

*My pastry chef, Mi Kyung Jeong, and I were brainstorming on how to make our red bean tiramisu tastier. We decided that coconut would make this pudding the star it wanted to be. Complemented with the nuttiness of misugaru, a popular grain powder, this tiramisu is one to swoon over, and quickly became a bestseller.*

## Serves 4–6

### CUSTARD BASE
100ml (3½fl oz) whole milk
150ml (5fl oz) whipping cream
2 large egg yolks
1 large egg white
75g (3oz) caster sugar
250g (9oz) mascarpone cheese
30g (1oz) misugaru
　(Korean roasted grain powder)

### CRUMBLE
115g (4oz) plain flour
35g (1oz) cocoa powder
100g (3½oz) desiccated coconut
a pinch of salt
135g (4½oz) unsalted butter, softened
135g (4½oz) caster sugar

### SPONGE FINGERS
180g (6oz) Italian sponge fingers
140ml (4¾fl oz) espresso, Italian style
50g (2oz) caster sugar
40ml (1½fl oz) white coconut rum

### TO ASSEMBLE
120g (3¾oz) canned sweetened whole
　adzuki beans
1 tbsp cocoa powder, mixed with
　1 tbsp misugaru
30g (1oz) coconut flakes, toasted

First, make the base, put the milk and cream in a saucepan set over a medium-low heat and bring to a gentle simmer, then set aside. In a separate bowl whisk the egg yolks, egg white and sugar until you have a light ribbon consistency. Pour a third of the warm milk and cream onto the eggs, whisking continuously. Pour the egg mixture back into the saucepan and whisk. Place over a medium heat, stirring continuously with a spatula until the temperature reaches 85°C (185°F) and you have a thick, creamy custard. Remove from the heat and tip the custard into a bowl set over an ice bath to cool immediately. Once cooled, pass through a fine sieve and store in the fridge until needed.

To make the crumble, combine the flour, cocoa, coconut and salt in a small bowl and set aside. In a stand mixer fitted with a paddle attachment, beat the butter and sugar until creamy. Reduce the speed to low and add the flour mixture gradually, beating until it becomes a dough. Gather the dough into a ball, wrap in clingfilm and let it rest in the fridge for 45 minutes. Preheat the oven to 175°C fan/195°C/365°F/gas 5 and line a baking sheet with parchment. Using a box grater, grate the dough into chunky pieces, then spread them evenly across the lined baking sheet. Bake for 8 minutes, then shake the tray to flip the pieces, then bake for 4 more minutes.

Place the sponge fingers on a flat tray. In a small bowl, mix the coffee, sugar, coconut rum and 55ml (2fl oz) water together and pour half of it over the fingers. Allow to soak for 1 minute, then turn the fingers over and pour over the remaining coffee mixture.

Place the chilled custard base, mascarpone and misugaru in a stand mixer and whisk on a medium–high speed for 3-4 minutes until creamy and light. Place half the soaked sponge fingers in the bottom of a serving bowl and spread half of the sweetened adzuki beans on top. Spoon half of the custard base on top. Place more soaked sponge fingers on the custard, add the rest of the adzuki beans, then cover with the remaining custard. Before serving, add a layer of crumble on top, then dust with the cocoa powder and misugaru. Sprinkle with toasted flaked coconut.

# SuJeongGwa Crème Brûlée

*SuJeongGwa, a persimmon, ginger and cinnamon tea, is usually served at the end a traditional meal. At my restaurant, we have kept this in mind, but offer it in the form of a classic French dessert rather than a sweet drink. Its sophisticated flavours make this crème brûlée taste royal.*

## Serves 6

250ml (8fl oz) whole milk
25g (1oz) ginger, peeled and thinly sliced
15g (½oz) cinnamon sticks, rinsed and broken into pieces
400ml (14fl oz) double cream
95g (3¼ oz) light brown sugar
7 egg yolks

### TO SERVE
5–6 tbsp caster sugar
1 persimmon, diced and tossed with sugar to taste
1 tbsp toasted pine nuts
4 tsp daechu (dried jujube dates)

Preheat the oven to 90˚C fan/110˚C/225°F/gas ¼.

Add the milk, ginger and cinnamon sticks to a medium saucepan set over a medium heat and simmer for 5 minutes. Remove the pan from the heat and set aside for 15 minutes to allow the mixture to infuse. Strain through a fine mesh sieve, then measure out 100ml (3½fl oz), discarding any excess.

Place the infused milk, cream and 60g (2½oz) of the brown sugar into a saucepan and bring to a simmer over a medium heat. In the meantime, place the egg yolks and the remaining sugar in a bowl and whisk until the sugar is dissolved. Once the cream mixture is simmering, remove from the heat and pour into the egg yolk mixture, a little at a time, to temper them. Once tempered, tip in the rest of the warm cream mixture and mix well using a spatula.

Strain the mixture through a fine sieve into a clean jug then pour the mixture into 4 individual brûlée dishes. Place the dishes in a roasting tray. Bake for about 30–40 minutes, or until the custard is set but still wobbles. Allow to cool at room temperature before placing in the fridge.

Just before serving, sprinkle a thin layer of caster sugar on top of the dishes. Using a blow-torch, gently caramelize the sugar. Alternatively, place the dishes under a hot grill until the sugar caramelizes. Garnish with the diced persimmon, toasted pine nuts and the daechu. Serve immediately as the sugar will start absorbing the moisture from the custard and go soft.

# Snickers Hotteok

*We launched my restaurant with this dessert and it has been the house favourite ever since. Hotteok, a flat stuffed doughnut, has always been my sister's most loved street food snack. Here, I have used the flavours of a Snicker's bar to make this version even more addictive.*

## Makes 12 hotteok

400ml (14fl oz) whole milk
20g (¾oz) fresh yeast, crumbled
  (or 11g (½oz) dried yeast)
50g (2oz) white sugar
1½ tsp fine salt
420g (14¾oz) plain flour,
  plus extra for dusting
180g (6oz) glutinous rice flour
30g (1oz) cornflour
2 eggs, lightly beaten
40g (1½oz) unsalted butter,
  diced and softened
vegetable oil, for cooking and greasing

FILLING
120ml (4fl oz) double cream
30g (1oz) whole milk
1½ tsp sea salt
245g (9oz) caster sugar
100g (3½oz) liquid glucose
20g (¾oz) unsalted butter,
  softened
100g (3½oz) peanuts,
  roasted and chopped
150g (5oz) dark chocolate,
  cut into 12 squares

To make the dough, warm the milk so that it's lukewarm and add the yeast. Make sure it is dissolved completely then set aside. Place the sugar, salt and flours in the bowl of a stand mixer and mix well with a large spoon. Add the warm milk and yeast and stir in. Start the mixer on medium speed with a dough hook attached. When it reaches a dough form, add the eggs in 3–4 additions, mixing well between each one. The dough will come away from the side of the bowl, and when it becomes elastic, add the diced butter a little at a time. When it is mixed, cover the bowl with a wet cloth and allow it to double in volume at room temperature. Press it down to knock the air out, then let it prove again in the fridge overnight, covered with a wet cloth and clingfilm on top.

For the filling, heat the milk and cream with the salt in a saucepan, then set aside.

To make the caramel, place the caster sugar and liquid glucose in a heavy-based pan over a medium heat until the sugar melts and becomes an amber colour. Add the butter, piece by piece, whisking each time to emulsify well. Add the warmed milk mixture to the caramel in stages, whisking each time. Finally add the peanuts and carry on cooking over a medium heat until the temperature reaches 116–117°C (240°F), stirring occasionally. Pour the caramel into a metal container and leave it to cool down completely. Once cool, wrap each chocolate square with 25g (1oz) of caramel, set on a greased baking sheet and reserve in the freezer.

Dust a clean work surface with flour and turn the dough out onto it. Dust the top of the dough with some more flour and knead it a few times. Cut the dough into twelve equal pieces, shape each piece into a ball, set on the floured work surface, and cover with clingfilm. Press a dough ball into a 10cm (4in) wide disc using your fingertips. Make sure the disc is uniformly thick so the finished hotteok will be evenly filled with caramel. Put the disc in your hand and cup it slightly.

Place the caramel-coated chocolate square in the centre of the disc, then seal the disc by wrapping the dough around the filling and pinching the edges together at the top. Once sealed, reshape gently to form a ball, set with the seam-side down on a greased baking sheet and cover with clingfilm. Repeat with the remaining dough balls and filling.

In a large, non-stick frying pan, heat 3 tablespoons of oil over a medium-high heat. Put two or three dough balls seam-side down in the pan and immediately flatten them with a spatula to a width of about 10cm (4in). Reduce the heat to medium-low and fry the hotteok for 3–4 minutes until golden brown and crispy on the bottom. Flip them and cook for a further 3–4 minutes until slightly springy to the touch.

Transfer the hotteoks to a wire rack or kitchen paper-lined plate when done. Repeat with the remaining dough balls, wiping the pan clean and adding fresh oil for each batch. Leave the hotteoks to cool slightly before serving. Beware, it's easy to burn yourself in your haste to gobble these up, as the insides are hot and oozing.

# Yuja Meringue Pie

*Yuja is one of my favourite ingredients from Korea, due to its gorgeous unique floral notes. If a bergamot lemon and a satsuma mandarin had a baby, it would be this ambrosial citron fruit. Using yuja here for this beloved pie elevates a humble dish to new heights.*

## Serves 6

### PASTRY
120g (3¾oz) unsalted butter, softened, plus extra for greasing
75g (3oz) icing sugar
1 egg, lightly beaten
seeds from ¼ vanilla pod
grated zest of ¼ lemon
200g (7oz) plain flour, plus extra for dusting
a pinch of salt

### YUJA FILLING
190g (6¾oz) caster sugar
¼ tsp agar agar
190ml (6½fl oz) yuja (yuzu) juice
grated zest of 1 lemon
3 large eggs
70g (2¾oz) unsalted butter, soft and diced

### MERINGUE
200g (7oz) caster sugar
1 tbsp liquid glucose
3 egg whites

For the pastry, in the bowl of a stand mixer fitted with a paddle attachment, beat the butter and icing sugar together until light and creamy. Add the egg in 3 additions, mixing well between each, then add the vanilla and lemon zest. When well mixed, add the flour and salt all at once. Beat on low speed and scrape down the sides of the bowl until the flour is evenly mixed. Gather the dough into a smooth, flat ball, wrap tightly in clingfilm and rest it in the fridge for 45 minutes.

Line a 23cm (9in) pie dish by greasing the sides and bottom with butter then dust with flour. Roll out the chilled dough on a lightly floured work surface and make a circle large enough to line the dish. As this is a very crumbly pastry, if it breaks you can just patch it together and mould it up the sides, making sure it is even all over. Trim off any excess pastry, then chill for another 30 minutes.

Preheat the oven to 165°C fan/185°C/365°F/gas 4½ and line the pastry case with parchment and fill with baking beans. Blind bake for 20–25 minutes until light golden brown. Remove the paper and baking beans and return the pie dish to the oven for another 10 minutes. Remove from the oven and allow it to cool completely.

To make the yuja filling, in a small bowl, mix 3 tablespoons of the sugar with the agar agar and set aside. Put the yuja juice and lemon zest in a saucepan, whisk in the agar mixture and bring to the boil, continuing to whisk. In a medium bowl, whisk the remaining sugar and eggs together, then gradually whisk in half of the yuja mixture to the egg mixture. Then, whisk this egg mixture back into the pan. Continue to whisk as you cook until the mixture is thick and bubbling. Remove from the heat. Stir in the butter and blitz with a stick blender. Pass through a fine sieve and pour the filling into the pastry case.

To make Italian meringue, place the eggs in the bowl of a stand mixer fitted with a whisk attachment and set aside. Pour 70ml (2¾fl oz) water into a heavy-based saucepan, add the sugar and liquid glucose and set over a medium heat. Bring to the boil, occasionally brushing down any crystals that form on the side of the pan, using a pastry brush moistened with water. Place the sugar thermometer in the boiling syrup. When it reaches 110˚C (230°F), start to whisk the egg whites on a medium-high speed. Stop cooking the syrup when it reaches 121˚C (250°F) and pour the syrup over the egg whites in a thin and steady stream. When all of the syrup has been added, increase the mixer speed to medium and continue to whisk until the meringue is almost completely cold.

Just before serving, spoon the meringue over the top of the pie to cover the filling. Wave a cook's blow-torch over the surface until the meringue is lightly tinged with brown, or place under a very hot grill for a few seconds. Keep chilled until ready to serve.

# Green Tea Roll Cake

*Asia is known for its love of rolled sponge cakes. Airy, light and fluffy, these pretty and often ornate logs are always a crowd-pleaser. I love the classic version, with green tea and fresh strawberries, and often serve this for afternoon tea as a great alternative to the traditional Victoria sponge.*

**Serves 6**

150g (5oz) plain flour
70g (2¾oz) green tea powder
  (matcha or garu nokcha)
½ tsp baking powder
½ tsp bicarbonate of soda
10 large eggs, separated and yolks
  lightly beaten
200g (7oz) caster sugar

JAM FILLING
1kg (2lb 4oz) raspberries
690g (1lb 9oz) caster sugar
2 tsp pectin powder
20g (¾oz) omija berries
  (schisandra) (optional)
juice of 1½ lemons

CREAM FILLING
500ml (16fl oz) double cream
120g (3¾oz) icing sugar
2 tsp green tea powder
  (matcha or garu nokcha)

TO FINISH
220g (7¾oz) strawberries, whole
matcha powder, for dusting
icing sugar, for dusting

Preheat the oven to fan 175°C/190°C/375°F/gas 5 and line a 43 x 29cm (17 x 11½in) baking tin with parchment and set aside.

Combine the flour, green tea powder, baking powder and bicarbonate of soda in a sieve and sift into a large bowl, then set aside. In a stand mixer with a whisk attachment, start to whisk the egg whites on low speed to aerate. Add the sugar and raise to a higher speed, and whisk until soft peaks form. Remove the bowl from the mixer and, using a rubber spatula, carefully fold the egg yolks into the meringue. In three additions, gently fold the sifted flour mixture into the meringue, taking care not to overmix. Pour the batter into the prepared baking tin and carefully smooth the top using a spatula. Bake for about 7 minutes, until the surface is golden brown and the centre springs back when lightly touched. Move the cake to a wire rack to cool.

For the jam, combine the raspberries and 625g (1lb 6oz) of the sugar in a medium heavy-based pan. Heat for a few minutes over a low heat until the sugar has dissolved and the fruit becomes soft. In a small bowl, thoroughly mix the pectin powder and the remaining sugar, then gradually stir this into the jam pan. Use a piece of cheesecloth to make a bag, place the omija berries inside and add the bag to the jam pan. Raise the heat to medium and clip a sugar thermometer to the side of your saucepan, with the end dipped in the boiling jam mixture. Bring to 105°C (220°F), stirring constantly and skimming off the foam. Once at the required temperature, remove from the heat, then whisk in the lemon juice. Set aside to cool for 10 minutes, then remove the bag and spoon into sterilized jars and seal with lids.

For the cream filling, place the cream, icing sugar and green tea powder in a bowl and whisk until soft peaks form. Keep in the fridge until needed.

To finish, spread the jam over the sponge, leaving a 2cm (¾in) gap around the edges. Spread the green tea cream over the top, again leaving the edges clear. Arrange the whole strawberries along the longest edge of the sponge. With parchment underneath, roll up the sponge tightly, making sure the filling stays inside. Roll the sponge off the parchment and dust with matcha powder and icing sugar. Cut into slices to serve.

# Makgeolli Panna Cotta

*I have had many nights imbibing makgeolli, Korea's fermented fizzy rice wine. Its sweet, yet tangy, effervescent flavour also lends itself to infusing into light, refreshing desserts. Makgeolli's unique piquancy is paired with tart passion fruit and yuja in this fragrant panna cotta recipe.*

## Serves 4

### PANNA COTTA

300ml (10fl oz) makgeolli
  (Korean rice liquor)
300ml (10fl oz) double cream
100g (3½oz) caster sugar
1 vanilla pod, seeds scraped
7g (¼oz) gelatine leaves,
  soaked in iced water to soften
200g (7oz) white chocolate
1½ tbsp yuja (yuzu) juice

### MANGO COMPOTE

2 ripe mangos
2 tsp fructose (fruit sugar)

### PASSION FRUIT AND YUJA JELLY

250g (9oz) yujacha
  (citron tea syrup)
3½ tbsp yuja (yuzu) juice
7g (¼oz) gelatine leaves,
  soaked in iced water to soften
pulp and seeds from 2 passion fruits

### SESAME SNAPS

150g (5oz) caster sugar
30g (1oz) black sesame seeds
70g (2¾oz) white sesame seeds
20g (¾oz) freeze-dried raspberries

First, make the mango compote. Peel and slice the mangos lengthways on either side of the stone. Discard the stone and dice the flesh into cubes. Coat the cubes with fructose, divide between four glasses and keep them in the fridge.

For the panna cotta, place the white chocolate and yuja juice in a large bowl and set aside. Shake the makgeolli then combine with the cream, sugar and vanilla seeds in a medium saucepan and place over a medium heat. Allow the liquid to come to a simmer, then remove from the heat. Squeeze the water from the gelatine, add to the saucepan and stir until completely dissolved. Pour the liquid onto the white chocolate and yuja juice then leave to stand for a couple of minutes. Blend with a stick blender for 2 minutes. Strain the liquid through a fine sieve and set aside, stirring occasionally until it becomes thick, like custard, as it cools down. Once it has thickened, pour the panna cotta mix into the glasses with the mango and chill in the fridge for about 3 hours, or until set.

For the passion fruit and yuja jelly, heat the yujacha and yuja juice in a small saucepan over a medium heat. Allow the liquid to come to a simmer, then remove from the heat. Squeeze the water from the gelatine and add it to the saucepan and stir until completely dissolved. Strain the liquid through a fine sieve, pressing down on the solids well. Discard the solids. Stir the passion fruit pulp and seeds into the liquid. Pour the jelly on top of each panna cotta, swirling the glass so the top is evenly coated. Allow to set in the fridge.

For the sesame snaps, cover a chopping board with two sheets of parchment and set aside. Put the sugar in a small heavy-based saucepan and heat for about 5 minutes on a medium heat to create a light caramel. Using a heatproof spatula, stir in the sesame seeds and freeze-dried raspberries and coat evenly with the caramel; the mixture will be clumpy. Spread it on the parchment and cover with the other sheet of parchment. Using a rolling pin, roll over the paper to flatten the sesame mixture as thinly as possible. Set aside to cool completely. Snap into pieces and serve alongside the panna cotta, and keeping any leftover in an airtight container.

# Asian Pear Tart

*When ripe, Asian pears are so much tastier than their Western counterparts. In Korea, I have travelled down to the city of Naju just to taste these sweet golden orbs fresh off the trees. My pastry chef, Mi Kyung Jeong, developed this unique pastry crust using buckwheat flour and sesame paste. It's divine!*

## Serves 8

150g (5oz) plain flour, plus extra for
   dusting
30g (1oz) wholemeal buckwheat flour
a pinch of salt
85g (3oz) butter, at room temperature
50g (2oz) caster sugar
½ large beaten egg
1 tbsp white sesame paste (or tahini)

### ALMOND CREAM FILLING

175g (6oz) unsalted butter, at room
   temperature
175g (6oz) caster sugar
3 eggs, lightly beaten
175g (6oz) ground almonds
40g (1½oz) plain flour

### TOPPING

2 Asian pears, peeled, halved and
   core removed. Cut 3 of the halves
   into 3 wedges, and thinly slice the
   remaining half
2 tbsp apricot jam or yujacha (citron tea
   syrup), mixed with 2 tbsp water
15g (½oz) flaked almonds, toasted

To make the pastry, in a small bowl, whisk the plain flour, buckwheat flour and salt together then set aside. In the bowl of a stand mixer fitted with a paddle attachment, beat the butter and sugar together on medium speed until well combined and fluffy. Reduce the speed to low, then add the egg and mix until fully combined. Add the sesame paste and mix in, then add the flour mixture and beat on low speed until the dough is formed. Gather the dough into a smooth flattened ball, wrap tightly in clingfilm and rest in the fridge for 45 minutes. (Alternatively, it can be frozen for use at a later date.)

Line a non-stick 23cm (9in) diameter, 4cm (1½in) deep loose-bottom fluted tart tin with parchment. Roll out the chilled dough on a lightly floured work surface to a circle large enough to line the tart tin, about 2mm (⅛in) thick. As this is a short, crumbly pastry, if it breaks you can simply patch it together in the tin and mould it up the sides, making sure it is even all over. Trim off any excess pastry, then chill for another 30 minutes.

Preheat the oven to 170°C fan/190°C/375°F/gas 5.

For the almond cream filling, using an electric mixer, beat the butter and sugar together on a medium–high speed until pale and light. Reduce the speed to low, add the beaten eggs in 3–4 stages, gradually and slowly, scraping down the side of the bowl with a rubber spatula after each addition, until completely incorporated. Add the ground almonds and flour and mix until the mixture is even. Then spread the filling evenly over the chilled pastry case.

Arrange the pear wedges in a circle, and in the middle, with the cut sides down and rounded sides poking out above the filling. Lift the tart tin onto a baking sheet and bake for 40–50 minutes until the pastry is golden and the filling is set. When it is done, transfer the tin to a wire rack to cool down, before removing the tart from the tin. Before serving, arrange the remaining pear slices on the top of the tart and brush with a hot apricot or citron tea syrup glaze and sprinkle with toasted flaked almonds. Serve warm or at room temperature.

# Sikhye Popsicles

*My mom used to make large jars of Sikhye that she'd leave to ferment in our laundry room. This sweet, malty and slightly cloudy rice drink is considered a digestive aid, and is usually served at the end of a large meal on festive holidays. Here, I have added some fun to tradition and transformed this classic elixir into a nostalgic popsicle.*

### Makes 12 popsicles

800ml (28fl oz) sikhye (rice punch)
1 tbsp yuja (yuzu) juice
2 tsp ginger juice
¼ tsp vanilla extract with seeds
1 punnet edible flowers

In a large bowl, combine the sikhye, yuja juice, ginger juice and vanilla extract and mix together. Transfer the mixture to a spouted measuring jug for easy pouring, then set aside.

Divide the edible flowers between twelve ice lolly moulds. Pour in the sikhye mixture to fill each mould, leaving about 5mm (¼in) space for expansion as it freezes. Assemble the covers and sticks for each mould.

Freeze the ice lollies for 4–5 hours until solid, before unmoulding.

# Miso Ice Cream

*Serve this on its own or with the Gochugaru and Nutella Brownie.*

### Makes 1.2 litres (2 pints)

450ml (15fl oz) whole milk
140ml (4¾fl oz) double cream
7 egg yolks
120g (3¾oz) light brown sugar
55g (2oz) white miso

To make the ice cream, put the milk and cream in a saucepan and bring to the boil gently; set aside. Whisk the egg yolks and sugar together to ribbon stage. Add one-third of the warm milk mixture to the eggs and sugar, whisking continuously, then pour the mixture back into the saucepan, whisking well. Place over a medium heat, stirring well until the temperature reaches 82°C (180°F). Remove from the heat and cool immediately by pouring into a clean container and placing the container in a large bowl of iced water. Stir occasionally to prevent a skin forming. When it's completely cooled, pass through a fine sieve, then add the miso and blitz with a stick blender until smooth.

Process the mixture in an ice-cream maker according to the manufacturer's instructions. Transfer the ice cream to a container with a tight-fitting lid and freeze to the desired firmness.

# Milkis and Elderflower Granita

*I grew up drinking so many of Korea's yummy soft drinks. Milkis, a fizzy, milky sweet soda, throws me right back to my childhood. This nostalgic and much loved, albeit slightly tawdry, pop drink shouldn't be shunned in later life. So don't turn up your nose, as I have reinvented it here in chic granita form, paired with the floral essence of elderflower.*

**Serves 6**

500ml (16fl oz) Milkis (carbonated milk
  and yoghurt flavoured beverage)
3 tbsp elderflower cordial

Mix the Milkis and elderflower cordial together and pour the mixture into a freezerproof glass or non-reactive baking dish. Transfer to the freezer, uncovered. After 3 hours, the granita should be slushy in the centre and icy at the edges of the dish. Use a fork to break it up and mix in the icier portions, pulling them to the centre of the dish. Return to the freezer for another 1–2 hours. Rake a fork over the surface and scrape to create flaky crystals. Return to the freezer and repeat as needed until the granita is light and fluffy. Cover with a lid or clingfilm until needed. Scoop the granita into ice-cold bowls to serve.

# Yakult Turkish Delight

*My mom used to freeze the small plastic Yakult bottles and my sister and I would peel off the thin plastic in round curly strips and suck on the sweet yoghurty ice greedily. This variation was inspired by the rose-flavoured 'Turkish delight' petit fours at one of the three-star restaurants I used to work at. This recipe is more like a jelly, and feel free to call it whatever you like, but these little mouthfuls are indeed 'delightful'.*

**Makes 60 cubes**

500ml (16fl oz) Yakult
17g (½ oz) gelatine leaves,
  soaked in iced water to soften
cornflour, for dusting

Line a 24.5 x 17.5 x 3cm (9½ x 7 x 1¼in) baking tray with a triple layer of clingfilm, then set aside.

In a small saucepan, warm up the 100ml (3½fl oz) of the Yakult over a medium heat; do not allow to boil. Remove the pan from the heat, add the gelatine and stir well until it is completely dissolved. Add the rest of the Yakult. Pour the liquid onto the tray and allow it to set in the fridge. Once firm, demould it, cut into cubes and coat them well with cornflour.

# Crunchy French Toast with Honey Butter Potato Chips and Mandarin Ice Cream

*The 'honey butter' craze in 2015 in Korea was real and practically caused mass hysteria. In this recipe, I have taken classic French toast and added a salty-sweet crunchy layer of honey butter crisps to make it even more decadent. Do try to find thick shokupan bread, as it makes a big difference in taste; if not you can use thickly sliced challah bread instead.*

**Serves 4**

4 slices shokupan (Japanese fluffy
  white bread) or challah
375ml (13fl oz) whole milk
60g (2½oz) caster sugar
5 eggs
2 tsp honey, plus extra to drizzle
finely grated zest of 4 mandarins
clarified butter, for frying
150g (5oz) honey butter crisps or lightly
  salted crisps, broken into crumbs

MANDARIN AND MILK ICE CREAM
450ml (15fl oz) whole milk
150ml (5fl oz) double cream
3 tbsp honey
90g (3¼oz) soured cream
180g (6¼oz) condensed milk
280g (10oz) mandarin (or orange)
  conserve

First, dry the bread out slightly, by wrapping the slices in clingfilm and refrigerating the slices overnight.

For the soaking liquid, combine the milk, sugar, eggs, honey and grated zest. Blitz with a stick blender, then refrigerate overnight to allow the flavour to infuse.

For the ice cream, in a large bowl blend the milk, cream, honey, soured cream and condensed milk together with a stick blender until it is well combined. Process the mixture in an ice-cream maker, according to the manufacturer's instructions. Transfer the ice cream to a container that has a tightly fitting lid. Add the mandarin conserve to the mixture by spreading it on top of the ice cream. Gently swirl with a butter knife then place the lid on the container and freeze to the desired firmness.

Remove the shokupan from the fridge, unwrap and place in a deep dish. Pass the soaking liquid through a sieve and pour it over the shokupan slices. Cover with clingfilm and place in the fridge for 15 minutes, then turn the bread over and soak for a further 10 minutes on the other side for the bread to soak up all the liquid.

Place the honey butter crisp crumbs on a plate and set aside. In a large non-stick frying pan, heat a generous amount of clarified butter over a medium heat. Press the soaked bread into the honey butter crisp crumbs on both sides and fry the bread for 3–4 minutes golden brown and crispy. Flip the slices and cook for a further 3–4 minutes until they are slightly springy to the touch.

Transfer the bread to a wire rack or kitchen paper-lined plate when done. Repeat with the remaining bread, wiping the pan clean and adding fresh butter for each batch. Leave the bread to cool slightly before serving with a scoop of mandarin ice cream and a drizzle of honey.

# Nurungji Rice Pudding

*I used to fight for the crispy layer of rice on the bottom of the rice cooker, that had caramelized nicely into a flat, round crisp perfect for snacking on. Now, you can buy this golden roasted rice 'cracker' in bags, capturing that toasted rice flavour, which makes for the most moreish rice pudding.*

**Serves 6**

800ml (28fl oz) milk
1 oksusu cha (roasted corn tea) tea bag
75g (3oz) pudding rice
150g (5oz) nurungji (scorched rice)
80g (3oz) caster sugar
50ml (2fl oz) double cream
200g (7oz) condensed milk
a splash of milk, if needed

TO SERVE
figs
nurungji, dusted in sugar
maple syrup

Put the milk and oksusu cha tea bag in a medium saucepan, bring to the boil gently, then remove the pan from the heat and let it infuse for 15 minutes.

Remove the tea bag and squeeze it out as much as you can to get the flavour. Add the pudding rice and nurungji to the same pan. Give it a good stir and bring to boil, then immediately turn the heat down to low. Cook gently for 30–40 minutes, stirring occasionally to ensure it does not catch on the bottom of the pan; the rice should be plumped up and tender. Add the sugar, cream and condensed milk and stir until it's soft, then remove the pan from the heat. Loosen the rice pudding with an extra splash of milk before serving, if needed.

Serve the rice pudding with figs, sugar-dusted nurungji and maple syrup drizzled on top.

# Gochugaru and Nutella Brownie

*I am a big fan of spiced Mexican-style chocolate. The mixture of chillies and chocolate balances out the sweetness and makes for a most surprising dessert. The heat of the gochugaru comes through at the end of every bite, a long, lingering complex flavour of warmth. You'll love it.*

## Makes 16 brownies

150g (5oz) plain flour
2 tsp table salt
3 tbsp gochugaru (Korean chilli flakes)
260g (9¼oz) caster sugar
1 tsp vanilla extract
4 eggs, at room temperature
300g (11oz) butter
245g (8¾oz) dark chocolate
  (54% cocoa solids), chopped
80g (3oz) whole hazelnuts
150g (5oz) Nutella, melted
Miso Ice Cream (page 203), to serve

HAZELNUT PRALINE
150g (5oz) hazelnuts
180g (6¼oz) caster sugar

Preheat the oven to 160°C fan/180°C/350°F/gas 4. Line a 20cm (8in) square baking tin with parchment.

To make the praline, roast the hazelnuts on a baking sheet for 15–20 minutes. Meanwhile, put the sugar in a saucepan set over a low heat. As the sugar melts, shake the pan from time to time. When it reaches an amber caramel, add the nuts and stir to combine. Tip the caramel onto a lined baking sheet and leave it to cool. Snap it into pieces and blitz to chunky crumbs in a food processor. Keep it in an airtight container.

Combine the flour and salt in a sieve and sift into a large bowl. Add the gochugaru and set aside. In another mixing bowl, whisk together the sugar, vanilla extract and eggs, then set aside.

To make the beurre noisette for the brownie, place the butter in a pan over a medium heat and bring to the boil. Cook until the butter stops bubbling, ensuring that it has turned a light golden brown (it should be around 155°C (310°F). Carefully pass it through a sieve and leave to cool for a few minutes.

Put the chocolate in a heatproof bowl and pour the warm beurre noisette over the chocolate, stirring until the chocolate is melted and smooth using a rubber spatula. Add the egg mixture to the chocolate in three stages, mixing well after each addition (if it looks split, blend it with a stick blender.) Add the flour mixture to the bowl in three stages, folding together gently.

Pour the batter into the prepared baking tin and sprinkle the whole hazelnuts over the top. Bake for 25–30 minutes, or until the edges appear crispy but a toothpick inserted into the centre comes out with moist crumbs (do not overbake).

Once baked, spread the melted Nutella on top and cover liberally with 80g (3oz) of the praline. Leave the brownies to cool at room temperature, then cut into squares. For best results, chill completely before slicing and serving with a scoop of miso ice cream.

# Aloe Vera Knickerbocker Glory

*Knickerbocker Glory is the British version of an American sundae. Usually made with strawberries, I opted for a green version of this fantastic dessert, showcasing aloe vera, pandan and green fruits, topped with a light dusting of green tea sugar and cookies.*

## Servces 4

### JELLY
350g (12oz) aloe vera juice drink
25g (1oz) caster sugar
15g (½oz) gelatine leaves, soaked in iced water to soften
grated zest of 1 lime
1 tbsp lime juice

### PANDAN SYRUP
40g (1½oz) pandan leaves, roughly chopped
50g (2oz) white sugar
1.5g (⅛ oz) gelatine leaves, soaked in iced water to soften
50g (2oz) Galia melon, puréed (use trimmings after dicing melon, see below)

### TO ASSEMBLE
300ml (10fl oz) whipping cream
¼ tsp vanilla extract with seeds
100g (3½oz) icing sugar
2 kiwis, cut into 3mm (⅛in) thick slices
½ galia melon, diced into 1½ cm (⅝in) cubes
½ bunch green grapes, each grape halved
400ml (14fl oz) vanilla or milk ice cream
1 star fruit, cut into 5mm (¼in) thick slices
4 green tea cookies, cut in half
4 green tea Oreo cookies, cut in half
8 green tea Pocky sticks

First, place the knickerbocker glory glasses in the freezer to chill.

To make the jelly, lightly grease a 17 x 24cm (6½ x 9½in) baking tray and set aside.

Put half the aloe vera juice and the sugar in a saucepan and warm gently. Add the softened gelatine leaves and let them completely dissolve in the liquid, then add the rest of the jelly ingredients including the rest of the aloe vera. Pour into the prepared tray and leave to set in the fridge.

To make the syrup, blend the pandan leaves with 75ml (3fl oz) water to form a paste. Squeeze the paste through a sieve so that you are left with an emerald-green liquid. Add the liquid to a small pan with the sugar, warm up above 50–60°C (122–140°F), add the soaked gelatine leaves and mix to dissolve in the syrup, then add the melon purée and blend them together. Tip the syrup into a bowl and place in the fridge to cool.

Place the whipping cream and vanilla extract in a bowl and whisk to soft peaks. Add the icing sugar and keep whisking until medium peaks. Transfer to a piping bag fitted with a star nozzle. Keep in the fridge until needed.

To assemble, divide the kiwi slices between the four glasses and line them against the inside of the glasses.

Cut the jelly into 1½cm (⅝in) cubes. Spoon some of the jelly cubes into the glasses, then add the diced melon, then the grapes. Top each glass with a large scoop of ice cream, then drizzle with some pandan syrup. Repeat until you've filled the glasses almost to the top. Top each one with a swirl of whipped cream and a final drizzle of pandan syrup, then garnish with sliced star fruit.

Garnish with the cookies and Pocky sticks into the top and serve.

# Oatmeal and Persimmon Daechu Bars

*American oatmeal bars are reminiscent of their British flapjack counterparts. When I was younger, I used to always make oatmeal bars for school bake sales to grand success. The dried persimmons and yujacha make a rather refined version of this grab-and-go snack. This easy-to-make bar was one of the most popular recipes on the book shoot!*

## Makes 16 bars

210ml (7fl oz) condensed milk
160g (5¾oz) dried persimmon,
  stems removed and sliced
90g (3¼oz) daechu (dried jujube dates),
  stoned and sliced
90g (3¼ oz) yujacha (citron tea syrup)
1 tsp yuja (yuzu) juice
240g (8½oz) butter, softened
245g (9oz) light brown sugar
2 tsp vanilla extract
110g (3¾oz) rice flour
1 tsp bicarbonate of soda
¼ tsp salt
300g (11oz) jumbo oats
120g (3¾oz) pecan nuts
80g (3oz) mixed seeds, nuts and
  dried berries (pumpkin seeds, sunflower
  seeds, pine nuts, goji berries, dried
  cranberries, dried blueberries)

Preheat the oven to 170°C fan/190°C/375°F/gas 5. Line a 33 x 23cm (13 x 9in) baking tin with parchment, letting some paper overhang the sides to act as handles; set aside.

In a saucepan, mix the condensed milk, dried persimmon, daechu, yujacha and yuja juice together. Bring to the boil, then remove from the heat immediately and set aside.

Using a stand mixer fitted with a paddle attachment, cream the butter, sugar and vanilla extract together until light and fluffy, about 5 minutes.

In the meantime, combine the rice flour, bicarbonate of soda and salt and sift into a large bowl. Whisk in the oats, pecans and mixed seeds, nuts and berries.

Add the flour and nut mixture to the butter mixture – this will form a crumbly texture. Add half of the condensed milk mixture, blend again until evenly combined, then set aside.

In the baking tin, spread the remaining condensed milk mixture over the bottom, then add the dough and press down evenly.

Bake for 25 minutes, then turn the tray and bake for a further 10–15 minutes. Set aside until it is cool, then remove from the pan and slice into sixteen bars. Store in an airtight container.

# Index

# Acknowledgements

Thank you so much firstly to Mi Kyung Jeong who co-authored this book with me.

MKJ      Your talent as a chef, attention to detail, and work ethic has been inspirational.
         It is an honor to have you on my team and to have you as a dear friend as well.
         I hope we have many more adventures together.

Thank you also to the whole Quarto team and the chefs who interned or came
to help on their days off: Bomi Jung (정 보미), Dana Choi (최 단아), Sol Gil Oh (오 솔길),
Hye Na Kwon (권 혜나), So Jeong Park(박 소정), Karol Dytkowski.

Thank you as well to all of my dear friends for all of your support. I have leaned on all
of you so many times and love and appreciate all of you for being you.

AEBH     As always my pillar and source of grounding and inspiration. I'm so lucky to
         have you as friends and colleagues. Thank you for standing by me.

JMS      You are a light to all, dear friend, and I'm so happy you entered my life.
         Thank you for your support and guidance.

HRD      Thank you for your friendship and showing me what it was like to feel alive again.

EAM      Thank you for your dear friendship and love over the years.

D & LG   Thank you for your friendship, warmth, love and support. Forever grateful.

GC & FL  I love all of our truly memorable adventures. Thank you for everything.

JG       Thank you never giving up on me and your passion.

ARS      So happy for you in this big year. May our girlie trips continue!

FJS      Love you and all of our amazing trips together.

SLP, POK, LLY, APW, ALW, KKC, VJ, JKC, FP, KB, SEP, RS, LHKC, NT, TL, KJH, JLB, SJS, JKB
         I love you all so much. Thank you for being there for me.
         I am blessed and honored to call you friends.

A huge thank you to H-Mart for their continued support and sponsorship.
www.hmart.com

Brimming with creative inspiration, how-to projects and useful
information to enrich your everyday life, Quarto Knows is a favourite
destination for those pursing their interests and passions. Visit our
site and dig deeper with our books into your area of interest:
Quarto Creates, Quarto Cooks, Quarto Homes, Quarto Lives,
Quarto Drives, Quarto Explores, Quarto Gifts, or Quarto Kids.

First published in 2019 by White Lion Publishing,
an imprint of The Quarto Group.
The Old Brewery, 6 Blundell Street
London, N7 9BH,
United Kingdom
T (0)20 7700 6700

www.QuartoKnows.com

Text © 2019 Judy Joo
Photography © 2019 Yuki Sugiura

© 2019 Quarto Publishing plc

A catalogue record for this book is available from the British Library.

UK ISBN   978 0 71124 210 4

US ISBN   978 0 71125 167 0

Ebook ISBN   978 0 71124 211 1

10 9 8 7 6 5 4 3 2 1

| | |
|---|---|
| **Comissioning Editors** | Melissa Hookway and Cerys Hughes |
| **Designer** | Isabel Eeles |
| **Editor** | Charlotte Frost |
| **Photographer** | Yuki Sugiura |
| **Production Controller** | Robin Boothroyd |
| **Publisher** | Jessica Axe |
| **Stylist** | Rebecca Woods |

Printed in China